Kings
on
the Rise

Kings on the Rise

Step Into Your Destiny of Kingship and Wealth-Building, Spearhead Kingdom on Earth

Wai-yee Schmidt

"I could not put this riveting book down. I read it through in one sitting! It is one of the most informative, captivating and motivating books on this subject I have ever read! Your identity will be transformed as you operate from a place of Kingship causing a paradigm shift towards wealth. I've personally spent time with Wai-yee over the years and have witnessed her success firsthand. If you've been looking for a clear step by step book on how to achieve success in finances even for beginners or experts, look no further. You've hit the jackpot!"

Dr. David Herzog, Best Selling Author and Speaker

Scottsdale, Arizona

www.thegloryzone.org

"Wai-yee Schmidt is a brilliant thinker, prolific investor and masterful thinker. She brings a potent new revelatory concept to life in these pages as she unpacks the destiny of Kings! Many of us are living far below our potential and this book provides the blueprint for the next level. It also gives needed instruction to prosper, enlarge, and embrace your unique Kingdom mandate. This is a must read for Kingdom leaders, investors, entrepreneurs and those who are passionate about destiny. Get ready to be challenged and motivated as you dive into this brilliant writing."

Dr. Ryan Lestrange, Apostolic Network Leader,

Best Selling Author and Speaker

Atlanta, Georgia

www.ryanlestrange.com

www.lestrangeglobal.com

KINGS ON THE RISE by Wai-yee Schmidt

ISBN (ebook): 979-8-9865707-1-6
ISBN (paperback): 979-8-9865707-2-3

Printed in the United States of America

Table of Contents

DOWNLOAD THE AUDIOBOOK FOR FREE!

Thank you for reading my book, Kings on the Rise. To say thanks, I would like to give you the Audiobook version for free.

Click the link below to download:

Kingsontherise.com

Acknowledgments

---◆---

I dedicate this book to Mario, my late husband, a major king in his time; my sons, Ryan and Simon, who are kings in the making; my spiritual parents, Apostles Ryan and Joy LeStrange; Pastor Morris Graves, Jr., of Sid Roth's ministry organization, Messianic Vision., Inc.,; Apostle David Herzog of David Herzog Ministries; investing buddies/brothers-in-arms like Apostle Cris Zimmermann and Christopher B. Smith; pillars of the KW Leadership Team, Annette Pacheco and Apostles Chris and Deb White; fellow kings and priests like Shawn Stiteler, Alan Marshall and Kevin W. Crystal; and finally, to many loved ones, trusted friends, prophets and intercessors who have inspired me infinitely for their unwavering support of the message to call out kings for Christ and build wealth for His kingdom. Here's to witnessing the rising of KINGS!

Foreword

From the very first time Wai-yee Schmidt began to explain the calling on her life to me, it was evident that God had placed a mantle on her that would have a significant impact on the church, on evangelism, and on the world. However, it wasn't until I began to read from the pages of this divine download that I truly began to understand the weight and magnitude of the incredible revelation this woman of God has received. Although I feel honored to have been amongst those who witnessed the finger of God that raised Wai-yee up and gave her a seat of influence at the table of some of the most elite investors in the world, halfway through this book I had to stop and repent to God for the years of refusing to wholeheartedly embrace the man of great spiritual influence God has anointed me to be. So, I pause to say thank you, Sister Wai-yee. I am convinced that Kings & Wealth will play a very significant role in the advancement of His glorious gospel. Through the diligent application of the principles of kingdom stewardship, this powerful woman of God has flourished financially as a global investor. Wai-yee possesses an uncanny ability to hear and trust God's voice and has therefore consistently seen God transform her divinely inspired theories into testimony.

I see Wai-yee's God-authored mandate as a twofold work. First, it is to challenge the household of faith to walk as heirs of God and coheirs with Yeshua the Messiah and as kings created with His King of kings' DNA to usher kingdom dominion onto this earth by taking territory in every sphere of influence. And second, it is to use her revelations as a tool for evangelism to whosoever wills as well. Throughout the corridors of time, the secular world has been using biblical principles to store massive wealth for the wicked. God is using the Kings & Wealth message to turn the system upside right, to elevate and overhaul mindsets, and to empower people to pursue godliness, excellence, and accomplishment. Essentially, readers will receive an impartation of the supernatural anointing to walk out the high calling of kings, take back territory for God, and create wealth for kingdom plans and purposes—an anointing that Wai-yee carries personally. This book is a powerful vehicle that will grant the reader personal access to the life-changing revelations that God downloaded to Wai-yee, while affording Wai-yee the opportunity to have a greater impact on God's kingdom people and a broader influence in the world for kingdom recovery and expansion. As you devour page after page of this God-inspired text, you will be enlightened, inspired, and empowered by the same divine impartation and God-given anointing for resources and wealth creation.

PASTOR MORRIS GRAVES JR, EZRA 7:10

Partner Relations Staff Pastor as ordained by Sid Roth of
It's Supernatural™ and Messianic Vision, Inc

Introduction

The Kings and Wealth revolution is personal. It started with my own journey, personal credentials of brokenness and scarring to qualify for this unique call on my life.

I spent my early years in a tiny apartment next to the cockroach-infested garbage chute of a building in Singapore's first public housing project. The housing project not only reeked of poverty and defeat but also was famous for housing the most notorious pedophiliac serial killers in the history of the island republic. The serial killers lived in the next building, about three hundred feet away from ours, while I was growing up in that neighborhood. In early 1981 they stuffed the body of a brutally raped and murdered nine-year-old girl in a bag and dumped it next to the elevator in my building, a mere thirty feet away from the door of our tiny apartment. Two weeks later the body of a ten-year-old boy was found nearby. Our family lived in that apartment till 1980, the year I turned ten, several months before the serial killers were arrested. Throughout my years in that neighborhood, I was blissfully unaware of and untouched by the evil brewing around me. It was as if God's hand was already shielding me.

This was my first childhood home, the place where my brother and I were left to fend for ourselves after school, day after day. My father was barely making ends meet but somehow managed to maintain a cash-burn lifestyle of drinking, gambling, and women. Occasionally he would show up drunk and invariably lash out at my mom or us. I grew up feeling angry and unloved. I threw myself into my studies, gaining a sense of achievement and accomplishment from academics, which paved the way for me to enter the prestigious and lucrative law profession.

I practiced as a corporate law/finance attorney for almost ten years in Singapore, Hong Kong, Beijing, and Frankfurt. I spent my first year in Hong Kong in a replica of my childhood home—a one-hundred-square-foot shoebox apartment with no windows—while making a lot of money as a first-year law associate and paying negligible taxes in the freewheeling, capitalist society of Hong Kong. I partied hard there and met my late husband, who was also a young attorney at that time.

I was quite a nut job for the Lord to work through by the time I got saved when I was twenty-four. My salvation story is seemingly unspectacular—I responded to an altar call at a wonderful church in Singapore. It was over a decade before I started walking in healing and wholeness amid a challenging marriage to another highly driven, overachieving, successful attorney while raising toddlers.

My healing journey began when I threw myself into studying again. This time it was not schoolbooks but *the* Book—the Word of God. The deeper I dove into His Word, the more healing and wholeness began to spread into my life, including my marriage and my family. We began to grow and prosper from the soul out, growing from strength to strength, glory to glory.

Beloved, I pray that you may prosper in all things and be in health, just as your soul prospers.

—3 JOHN 1:2

I began leading Bible study at church. I also started venturing into an everyday type of evangelism, sharing the gospel with whomever the Lord brought across my path and baptizing in my bathtub those who got saved. God confirmed His Word as I stepped out in bold and uncommon faith. What started as theory became a powerful testimony of the truth.

As we prospered spiritually, we also began to flourish financially through the diligent application of kingdom stewardship principles I learned through studying the Word. Over the past decade my late husband and I built a multimillion-dollar real estate portfolio consisting of rental properties and a flipping business in which I remodeled and sold small apartments for profit. I also taught myself to invest in the stock market over the past four years and earned returns matching those of professional money managers. Theory was again transforming into testimony as we continually stepped out in uncommon faith.

At the end of 2017 I sensed a shift coming for my ministry—I was no longer to focus on spontaneous evangelism, touching a few souls here and there in my city of Frankfurt. Instead, I had a new mandate. I was to use my professional/business DNA to teach the body of Christ to pursue excellence and accomplishment, and I was to impart the God-given supernatural anointing for resource and wealth creation. But more importantly I was to teach and impart revelations on the core identity and design of our spiritual DNA, which should undergird every endeavor in our lives as the sons and daughters of the Most High.

As I was putting together the pieces of my new mandate, I was conflicted, as it meant I had to be vulnerable and open about our lives and the personal stewarding of our finances. I was being asked by God to teach on a highly controversial topic. Teaching on finances or wealth is often mischaracterized as "prosperity teaching" and is therefore taboo. I felt as if I were volunteering to have a target on my back for the armies of online trolls and religious churchgoers who are quick to attack those who even dare to teach on wealth. Yet the lies perpetrated have held many believers in captivity for generations, resulting in their being blind to biblical truths and being perpetually broke, their true identities stolen, and their inheritances robbed.

The Lord then posed to me the same question posed to Queen Esther: "Who knows whether you have come to the kingdom for such a time as this?" (Esther 4:14).

You see, just as Esther was elevated to royalty for a purpose—to save her people from destruction—God elevated my family to our level of resource and abundance for a purpose. Although enjoying the fruits of our labor was not wrong, keeping the secret of our success to ourselves was. God's plan for us was bigger. My journey of redemption and abundance put His glory on full and spectacular display.

For a few weeks I kept hearing one word in my spirit: *groundswell*. It means "a rapid spontaneous growth."[11] It was time for some rapid growth. It was time for believers to break out of old thought patterns by adopting a new grid of foundational truths that would rebuild their thought processes and identities.

In November 2017 I released the message of kingship for the first time at a local church in Frankfurt at which I was invited to preach. The message had immediate resonance.

The Launchpad Visions

Not long after I first taught the message of kingship, I had three visions that helped launch the Kings and Wealth message.

In early 2018 I had a dream triggered by what I saw in the stock market, and I published my first article on wealth transfer on January 17. I wrote that I believe the great and elusive wealth transfer promised in the Bible was about to begin.[2] Right after the day the article was published, I had my first of the three launchpad visions.

Vision 1: The Casting of the Crowns

Jesus was wearing a long golden robe, studded with gems and precious stones. There was a boundless crowd standing before Him. Revelation 19:12 says of Jesus that "on His head were many crowns," and in my vision He was casting many crowns out to the masses. There were crowns for business owners, real estate agents, developers, stock market traders, bankers, builders, tech innovators, medical professionals, engineers, artists, scientists, musicians, beauticians, educators, curators, and even government leaders and politicians.

However, many of these crowns fell to the ground, by the wayside, and into puddles of mud. Most in the crowd were either dodging the crowns flying toward them, or standing frozen, looking like deer in headlights. Only one or two courageously lunged forward to catch their crowns.

The Lord revealed that most were paralyzed because they felt unworthy of the gem-studded crowns. They didn't think they were good enough to assume the identity of kings. The few who caught their crowns started picking up the other crowns and collected as many as they could, the way little kids pick up candy fallen from a birthday piñata.

Nine months later, in October 2018, I received two more visions while on a tour in Israel with David Herzog Ministries.

Vision 2: The Coronation and the Battlefield

When I was in Jerusalem, the moment I physically placed my hands on the Western Wall, I saw rows of golden crowns studded with gems, diamonds, and pearls. I also saw a long line of kings getting ready for the coronation. I heard pulsating drums, flutes, and music fit for a king's procession. In an instant, the coronation scene switched to a battlefield where there was massive blood-letting—the kings were warring, battling to conquer and take territory victoriously.

Vision 3: Release of Blueprints and Dark, Secret Places Revealing Hidden Riches

One of the key tour stops was in Bethel on October 3, 2018. While I was there, I experienced an open heaven portal firsthand. As soon as I laid my head down on a flat rock, a myriad of flickering, fast-moving images rushed at me.

I saw a massive temple with enormous steps paved in gold leading up to it. Then I saw an army of kings not only draped but dripping in gold. They were ascending the massive steps and heading toward the temple.

Jesus was crowned and dressed in gold. Blueprints were rapidly being handed out to the kings, one after another. I was Jesus' little helper, standing right next to Him, helping Him hand out those blueprints. Books, volumes, instructions, and strategies were being distributed. Suddenly there was again a switch of images. I saw calculators appearing and floating in pitch-black darkness, with hands typing on them furiously. Later on, I was reminded of the passage in the Bible that explains this odd vision:

> I will give you the treasures of darkness and hidden riches of secret places, that you may know that I, the LORD, who call you by your name, am the God of Israel.

> —ISAIAH 45:3

Through the visions God gave me, a message has been emerging, crystallizing, and evolving. I am scratching the surface and uncovering small parts of the tapestry God is weaving. I believe this is the beginning of a revolution not only to reverse generational bondages into generational blessings, but to mobilize and awaken a tribe of sleeping giants, a revolution birthed in the heart of God.

PART I
KINGS

Before we jump into the thick of the material, let's take a step back as I want to pose this question to you personally: Are you ready to make the sacrifices and pay the price to go on this journey with me, to live out your fullest God-ordained potential—that is, to be a king? If not, simply put this book down or pass it on.

You will learn about God's intended core design and identity for kings and new mindsets. For the sake of candor, a mindset transplant is mandated so you are equipped to operate like a God-sanctioned king, with a godly push and appetite to conquer and take territory, studying standards that you have never attained before so that you have the tools to reach for them after this book, with the eventual objectives to bring reform, kingdom dominion, and advancement on earth.

Just as death and taxes are certain in life, the pain involved in this process of transformation is just as certain. But I can assure you, coming out on the side of victory for yourself, your descendants, and the kingdom will more than compensate you for the sacrifices you make on this journey in collaboration with the King of kings.

CHAPTER 1

The Call to Raise Kings, Recover Lost Ground, and Restore Wealth to the Kingdom

The transfer of wealth has begun. Are you a participant or is it passing you by?

W hen was the last time you heard someone in Christian circles refer to himself as a king? How many believers do you know who have the confidence to view themselves as kings?

Truth be told, the clan of kings is like the lost tribe of Benjamin—nowhere to be found in the body of Christ. The enemy has obliterated the identity of believers as kings by carpet-bombing them with feelings of defeat, failure, lack, and unworthiness, which explains the scene in my first vision in which many refused to catch the crowns cast to them by Jesus. Other believers who have succeeded and prospered as kings in the world stay hidden, fudging their Christian identity in the workplace. Truth be told, I catch myself doing the same thing every so often when moving daily among investor circles.

The concept of winning has been lost in church. Verbiage such as "How do Christians succeed in the world?" rarely makes an appearance from the pulpit. With all due respect to clergy, oftentimes this is due to the lack of knowledge and/or experience of church leaders, who are mostly educated at Bible colleges, not business schools. More often than not, themes such as winning and success are frowned upon as facilitating a prideful spirit.

The failure of the body of Christ to take on secular leadership and to win in the world is a direct contravention of Genesis 1:26, where man is mandated by God to have dominion over everything on the earth:

> Then God said, "Let Us make man in Our image, according to Our likeness; let them have dominion over the fish of the sea, over the birds of the air, and over the cattle, over all the earth and over every creeping thing that creeps on the earth."

Revelation 1:6 says He has made us *kings* and priests:

> [He] has made us kings and priests to His God and Father, to Him be glory and dominion forever and ever. Amen.

Revelation 5:10 goes further to mandate that we shall reign on the earth:

> [You] have made us kings and priests to our God; and we shall reign on the earth.

By not accepting the mandate to have dominion over the earth as kings, the church keeps losing ground in influence, relevance, and wealth accumulation in the world in which we live. The body of Christ has been left behind during the extreme growth and rapid advancement taking place in our world in the last century.

I came to the realization the church was being left behind when I heard Lance Wallnau expound brilliantly on the seven-mountain mandate. The seven mountains are seven "molders of culture" or seven "world kingdoms." The church has been so focused on the church mountain that it has neglected to ascend to the top of the other six mountains: education, family, government, media, arts/entertainment, and business/finance. But to reap the harvest of nations, the body of Christ needs to climb to the top of all seven mountains.[1]

When the Lord birthed this unique assignment in me to call out those appointed to be kings, it became clear that believers have copped out on their calling as leaders in their God-appointed spheres of influence. Believers must be courageous and step into their callings as kings, and they must battle, they must win, and they must *recover lost ground,* and take back the world for Jesus, the King of kings. This concept ties in with the bloody battlefield in the second vision.

Once kings begin to flourish in their true identities and callings and they implement the blueprints handed to them from heaven, as seen in the third vision, wealth will both naturally and supernaturally flow through their hands and into the kingdom of God. The greatly anticipated transfer of wealth will finally be jump-started and no longer be just biblical "mythology."

> For behold, the darkness shall cover the earth...the LORD will arise over you, and His glory will be seen upon you. The Gentiles shall come to your light, and kings to the brightness of your rising....Then you shall see and become radiant, and your heart shall swell with joy; because the abundance of the sea shall be turned to you, the wealth of the Gentiles shall come to you....They shall bring gold and incense, and...proclaim the praises of the LORD....Therefore your gates shall be open continually; they shall not be shut day or night, that men

> may bring to you the wealth of the Gentiles, and their
> kings in procession.
>
> —ISAIAH 60:2–3, 5–6, 11

Events in the real-world economy moved at an accelerated pace even as I wrote Part I. In February 2020 the Trump administration was considering making it possible for Americans to invest a portion of their household income in the stock market on a tax-free basis.[2] Robinhood, a popular online trading platform, added three million investor accounts, half of which were for first-time investors, in the first five months of 2020, right in the midst of COVID-19 volatility in the stock market.[3] Many Robinhood investors have outperformed institutional investors in 2020.[4] On June 9, 2020, the Nasdaq Composite hit a historical high of 10,000.[5] I actually took a screenshot that day at the appointed second, showing the Nasdaq at 10,000.77 and up 0.77%, as the impossibly precise numerals of 10 and 7 flashed across my screen. The Holy Spirit was clearly showing off His spectacular work of art, and I captured it. Since July, the Nasdaq has shot past 12,000 (as of November 2020).[6]

On January 17, 2018, my article entitled "The Transfer of Wealth, the Stock Market and the Clarion Call for the Body of Christ" was published on Elijah List. In this article I mentioned President Trump's prediction of the Dow Jones Index hitting 30,000 one day.[7] Almost three years later, on November 24, 2020, the Dow Jones Index burst through 30,000 for the first time ever, a milestone in the history of the stock market, fulfilling the President's prediction.[8] At the time of writing that article, the Dow was around 25,000 in January 2018. Since then, the Dow moved 5,000 points to the upside, ironically in the year of the pandemic.

The greatly anticipated wealth transfer has already begun. My question to you is, are you a participant or is it passing you by? Do you want to participate? Are you ready to take a deep dive with me?

CHAPTER 2

Kings' Core Design

We have the DNA of Jesus, the DNA of KINGS! That is our source code.

In mid-February 2020 the US Justice Department indicted the Chinese telecommunications conglomerate Huawei on charges of misappropriating, or stealing, sophisticated technology from US companies, including trade-secret information and copyrighted works, such as source code and robot testing technology.[1] The theft of source code was one of the actions that triggered this huge clampdown by the US authorities. So, what is source code? Why were US authorities so ticked off that they would risk further tensions with China after two tumultuous years of trade war?

In the tech world, source code contains the commands that run computer programs; that is, the architectural platform code of a computer program. The platform code contains what tech industry people call declarations and loops. These declarations and loops dictate how the program functions. The source code of a computer program is akin to a human's DNA. Huawei's theft of intellectual property is important as the source code is seen as an act of aggression posing a threat to national security and interests.

The source code for human beings is the DNA. Your DNA dictates how you function. So, what is revealed by an analysis of your source code, your spiritual DNA, your core design?

Your core design, your source code, began with God's original plan for mankind before the fall. Genesis 1:26–27 states unequivocally, "'Let Us make man in Our image, according to Our likeness....' So, God created man in His own image; in the image of God He created him; male and female He created them." This concept of reproduction and replication is repeated in the New Testament, as a specific event which we call *being born again*. This occurs when a person decides to make Jesus his Lord and Savior, upon which the person becomes what the Bible refers to as a *new creation* (2 Cor. 5:17) and has a new life.

Romans 6:4–5 says, "We also should walk in newness of life. For if we have been united together in the likeness of His death, certainly we also shall be in the likeness of His resurrection." The words "united together" do not do justice to the Greek translation of these two words. In Greek, it is *symphytos*. *Symphytos* possesses a far more profound meaning than just a superficial understanding of *union*. It means "born together with, of joint origin...grown together...grown along with...planted together."[2]

First Corinthians 6:17 further states, "He who is joined to the Lord is one spirit with Him." This reinforces an inviolable, immutable truth that you are wired genetically in your *spirit* to be one with Jesus, to be identical with Him. Note that you are of the same origin, or nature, as Jesus—not just made in His image, like a reflection in the mirror that's only a shadow of the real thing. When you were born-again, you became a newly created spirit being who possesses the DNA of Jesus Christ Himself.

That's mind-blowing, don't you think—that you possess the DNA of Christ Himself and therefore you are exactly, 100 percent, like Him in your newly created spirit being? Yet 1 John 4:17 confirms the concept crisp and clear:

As He is, so are we in this world.

But let me throw another massive mind grenade at you. Jesus has many titles, one of which is "ruler over the kings of the earth" (Rev. 1:5). He is the true King, the King of kings (Rev. 17:14). So not only do you possess His DNA, but also you have the DNA of kingship, since Jesus is the King of kings. The word *kings* in Jesus' title are often understood as meaning earthly kings and politicians, meaning Jesus rules over earthly leaders and politicians. While that might be valid, I believe it is too narrow an interpretation. I believe the plural *kings* refer to believers being His 'Mini-Mes', His reproductions, or offspring, carrying His kingship DNA. You and I are created to be His kings on earth, to arise, lead, rule, and reign alongside Him (Rev. 5:10). Ephesians 2:6 declares, "In our union with Christ Jesus [God] raised us up with him to rule with him in the heavenly world" (GNT).

The name of this whole teaching, Kings On The Rise, is predicated on this lynchpin verse in the Book of Revelation:

[Jesus] has made us kings and priests to His God and Father, to Him be glory and dominion forever and ever. Amen.

—REVELATION 1:6

He has made us kings and priests. I can't reiterate this enough. We are not programmed or conditioned to believe or receive what I am saying. Try saying out loud that you are a king. Just say, "I am a king." How does it feel, weird and unfamiliar? Do you feel undeserving of such a title? Do you feel prideful? How dare you call yourself a king!

That is exactly what the enemy wants you to think and feel, but it cannot be further from the truth. When you think and feel things that don't line up with the truth of the Word, it is by courtesy of the enemy, whose plan is and ever was to systemically deceive, belittle, and destroy you from the moment you were conceived in your mother's womb.

Your core design is that of a king. Your source code is the DNA of a king because Jesus Himself is King, and multiple verses repeat this singular truth—you are one with Him and therefore, a 'KING'.

Core Mandate

You were created to be a king, and as a king you also have a mandate:

[You] have made us kings and priests to our God; and we shall reign on the earth.

—REVELATION 5:10

Genesis 1:28 also spells out your mandate in a crystal-clear fashion:

Then God blessed them, and God said to them, "Be fruitful and multiply; fill the earth and subdue it; have dominion over the fish of the sea, over the birds of the air, and over every living thing that moves on the earth."

Let me use another tech term, *default factory setting*, as an analogy. This should be more familiar. You know how you can reset your phone to its default factory settings when it gets a little out of whack? Genesis 1:28 is our default-factory-setting mandate: to be fruitful, to multiply, to fill the earth, to subdue the earth, and to have dominion over everything—paraphrased as -- to reign and rule on earth alongside Christ.

I am truly fascinated with the Holy Spirit's choice of the word *subdue*. The word *subdue* is neither polite nor politically correct. Neither is the word *dominion*, for that matter. The original Hebrew word for *subdue* is *kabash*. It means "to bring into bondage, make subservient…subjugate…force, keep under, subdue, bring into subjection."[3] To me *kabash* sounds not only powerful but also violent by any standard, especially in our day and age, when hypersensitivity to political correctness abounds. The Hebrew word for *dominion, radah,* is similar. It means "to tread down, i.e., subjugate…have dominion, prevail against, reign…rule."[4]

Yet these are the words God chose to use to convey His mandate to you and me as kings—to conquer, rule, reign, bring into bondage, and subdue the earth and everything in it. In fact, we can read further into Genesis 1:28 as God giving man authority to conquer all physical dimensions of His creation—water, land, air, and even space. Over the centuries, we have seen man's innate desire to conquer the seven seas through ships and submarines, conquer land through the auto industry, conquer the air through the power of aviation, and even conquer the final frontier, space, through space shuttles and rockets. In 2022, SpaceX, a commercial enterprise founded by Elon Musk, successfully launched two astronauts safely into orbit, making SpaceX the first private company to send astronauts to the International Space Station. This feat illustrates what God has placed in the heart of mankind—the desire to conquer, rule, and subdue.

Taken from another angle, there is another simple and obvious explanation to all this. God Himself is the Ruler and Creator; since we were made in His image, we too are rulers and creators. God's intrinsic nature is to create, to own, to reign, to rule, to legislate, to govern, and to bring order to the universe He created. We have been mandated by God to do the same.

One sidebar: I have been asked frequently why I do not refer to the ladies as queens. To clarify, kingship is a gender-neutral reference. It's God's nature and DNA that we have inherited, that of the King of kings. The kingly mantle and anointing we have inherited has nothing to do with gender, but everything to do with the ruling and reigning mandate of the King of kings. Further, Jesus called us to be kings and priests, not kings, queens, and priests.

Core Traits

I am convinced that every king possesses certain core traits. While not an exhaustive list by any means, here are some key core traits of kings:

- genius by design
- exceptional clarity of vision
- strategy and tenacity to triumph over trials

Genius by design

There has always been an ongoing debate as to whether intelligence is an outcome of nature or nurture or both. Multiple kinds of intelligence exist, ranging from logical to musical to spatial to interpersonal to intrapersonal to naturalist to linguistic to bodily-kinesthetic, something that professional athletes often possess.[5] For instance, Michael Jordan clearly possesses genius-level bodily-kinesthetic intelligence in basketball, and I personally view the founders and CEOs of big tech companies—like Elon Musk of Tesla, Jensen Huang of Nvidia and Jeff Bezos of Amazon as the most outstanding geniuses of today.

Musk is particularly brilliant and fascinating all at once. He was born and raised in South Africa. He's responsible for several successful revolutionary tech businesses. Most people do not have the capacity to build one successful business, let alone several. SpaceX was founded by Musk in 2002. He also founded X.com, an online banking company that eventually merged with another company and became PayPal. Through the PayPal digital platform, global payments can occur in a matter of seconds with minimal expense, which was unthinkable back in the day. He has also been the CEO of Tesla since 2008. He clearly is a genius by any metric .

While there are multitudes of complex theories as to why people are intelligent, the biblical position on the subject is, in contrast, simple and straightforward. I am convinced that every person called to be a king has the potential of genius deposited inside of him or her because it is the full intention and design of God to inject His wisdom and intelligence into us. First Corinthians 1:27 unapologetically states His intention and divine plan as such:

But God has chosen the foolish things of the world to put to shame the wise, and God has chosen the weak things of the world to put to shame the things which are mighty.

—1 CORINTHIANS 1:27

This is great news for those of us who have been called worthless or stupid while growing up. God can't wait to use you to outperform those considered wise in the eyes of the world. How will you outperform the world and shame the wise? You have an asset that the world doesn't—the mind of Christ.

We have the mind of Christ.

—1 CORINTHIANS 2:16

As a born-again believer, you have the mind of Jesus Christ! Earlier in the same chapter that tells us we have the mind of Christ, the apostle Paul discussed at length that God has revealed to us the deep things of God through His Spirit:

"Eye has not seen, nor ear heard, nor have entered into the heart of man the things which God has prepared for those who love Him." But God has revealed them to us through His Spirit. For the Spirit searches all things, yes, the deep things of God.

—1 CORINTHIANS 2:9–10

I believe verse 10 explains verse 16 and what it means to

have the mind of Jesus Christ Himself. Here is the Amplified Bible translation of verse 10:

> For God has unveiled them and revealed them to us through the [Holy] Spirit; for the Spirit searches all things [diligently], even [sounding and measuring] the [profound] depths of God [the divine counsels and things far beyond human understanding].

> —1 CORINTHIANS 2:10 AMP

By authority of this scripture, God has shared with you and me, albeit mere mortals, His divine wisdom and secrets that are inexplicable and immeasurable in depth and breadth through His Spirit dwelling in us.

Here's a hot-off-the-press, blow-your-mind testimony to demonstrate the truth and power of this verse. On November 18, 2020, while I was updating my presentation slides for the Kings & Wealth Online Conference 2020, the very second, I came to read these verses, "'Eye has not seen, nor ear heard....' But God has revealed them to us through His Spirit," I heard a still, small voice saying to me, "Check your stock portfolio now!" That was around 9:45 p.m. in Germany, and the stock market in New York was about to close in fifteen minutes. I quickly logged into my portfolio account and saw that my Tesla stock had popped over 20 percent after being left for dead for more than two months. I quickly exited my position in Tesla by selling all my shares. In that ten-minute window, I was able to take a huge profit off the table. I would have missed that window of opportunity if the Holy Spirit hadn't revealed it to me in such a timely manner.

If you are a born-again believer of Jesus Christ, God has already given you the mind of Christ through His Spirit in you. This means you can theoretically access God's secrets and counsel in a way an ordinary human who is not born-again and therefore does not have His Spirit, cannot.

Having the mind of Christ in you becomes the ultimate equalizer in life. Consider this statement carefully because it has huge implications: a believer with a supposedly naturally low IQ still possesses the same spiritual DNA as that of a believer with a naturally high IQ. They both have the same spiritual DNA, the DNA of Jesus Christ, in them. As far as I am concerned, having the DNA of Christ is equivalent to having genius operating software program installed in them. That means both believers have the same potential to be a genius.

My fellow kings, my intention here is not to shame you but simply to highlight the obvious and jolt you into clarity. The promise that you have the mind of Christ invalidates any lame excuse you might give yourself for your failures or inadequacies. Is there anything you cannot learn or master if you have the mind of Christ? Is there any king in the world that you cannot outperform as you walk out the calling of God on your life? Isn't it clear that His intention and design is to use you to shame the wise of the world for His glory and that He has even equipped you with the tools necessary to do so? Each of us has the makings of greatness inside us.

With the pandemic lockdown in 2020, I am unabashed to confess that I was happily bingeing on a few Netflix series, among them a culinary competition show called *The Final Table*; a glassblowing competition show called *Blown Away*, allowing me to discover a new art form; dystopian stories such as *Utopia*, in which rich, intricate plots unfold like layers of an onion; or to be sucked into Willy Wonka's wacky world with my kids. I recall being upset with myself for the bingeing, thinking I needed more deliverance ministry! But it wasn't just for entertainment or escape. It was because I was attracted to genius. When we experience genius, we are getting a glimpse of God and His deity. We experience genius on full display with the top chefs in heated competition or brilliant storytelling that transports us to another universe. We are watching genius at work, and we want more. In fact, we all are admirers of the work of the weird, the quirky, and the brilliant. As I watched and witnessed the genius of ordinary people in action, it reinforced my theory that if God imparted so much genius to them, it is even more His design to deposit His genius in believers.

I think a line from the movie *Where'd You Go, Bernadette*—starring Cate Blanchett as a brilliant architect who lost her way—sums up the importance of tapping into your genius design. That one line in the movie left me lost for words:

> **People like you [creative geniuses] must create. If you don't…, you will become a menace to society.**[6]

Boom! It's a drop-the-mic moment.

Friends, it's time. No more flimsy, lame excuses for failures or inadequacies. Instead of merely watching genius in action, it's time for believers to put their genius into action. God wants to use you to succeed and outperform the world.

Exceptional clarity of vision

It's one thing to have vision; it's another to have exceptional clarity of vision that can facilitate fruition. *A vision is only as good as cotton candy when it is unfulfilled—all fluff and sugar with no substance.* Kings must have exceptional clarity of vision to see a project through. The single-mindedness to execute their vision is what sets successful kings apart. Their ability to lock in on their goals and never lose sight of them brings them across the finish line.

When we bought our house in 2013, my architect and I spent six months just planning and getting construction permits. The construction was completed in merely six months. I had a vision with exceptional clarity, including the smallest details—from the color of the tastefully muted gold wallpaper, to the bathroom walls covered with a turquoise glass mosaic with specks of gold woven through to create the look of glistening ocean waves in landlocked Frankfurt, to the custom layout of the master bedroom to optimize storage in awkward attic spaces, to the strategically placed bay window that not only was the perfect nook for me to study the Bible and spend time with the Lord but also triggered the purchase impulse of the people who bought the house from me. I recall how my architect would say sternly in exasperation, "Frau Schmidt, I cannot see what is inside your head!" I had such clarity and detail in my head of how I wanted the house to look, and we worked tirelessly and relentlessly to manifest my vision. We spent over a million euros stripping, gutting, expanding, and reconstructing the house. We transformed a charming but neglected 1930s German brick villa with an overgrown, unkempt garden into a luxury piece of real estate, a secluded, idyllic green oasis in the middle of a bustling city. When I released the house for sale in an 'off-market', pocket listing in November 2019, I received a full price offer in less than two weeks.

The Bible says, "Where there is no vision, the people perish" (Prov. 29:18, mev). It also says, "Write the vision and make it plain on tablets, that he may run who reads it" (Hab. 2:2). Kings must not only have clarity of vision but also the ability to communicate that vision to others.

Strategy and tenacity to triumph over trials

The global pandemic also decimated much of the global economy. As governments around the world shuttered entire economies in 2020 to slow the spread of the Covid-19 virus,[7] millions of job losses were caused not seen since the Great Depression.[8] Entire industries relating to domestic and international travel, hospitality, and food service were wiped out. Many international borders remain closed at the time of writing Part I in 2020. Now in 2022, with the global economy re-opening, we are faced with unprecedented supply chain issues, inflationary pressures, and coupled with the Ukraine war, energy and commodity prices are higher than ever before. The world has never experienced a consecutive series of unexpected crises of such nature or proportion. But amid this mayhem, God's Word remains the final authority for us as believers to shape the outcome of our individual fates:

Now thanks be to God who always leads us in triumph in Christ.

—2 CORINTHIANS 2:14

An innate ability to bulldoze through adversity and end up with the upper hand is what sets kings apart. In fact, facing adversity can spur a person to fight even harder. Watching Michael Jordan in *The Last Dance* was awe-inspiring. It was intriguing to see how he was able to latch on to something that was working against him and use that to propel him toward victory during the game, whether it was a coach on the other team slighting him or a player talking trash about him.

The Bible is also full of examples of those with the tenacity to triumph over trials. Jacob was scammed by his own father-in-law, Laban, and spent twenty-one years laboring for him. (See Genesis 30–31.) Yet Jacob never resigned himself to serving Laban for the rest of his life. In fact, he rose above his dire circumstances and made a daring bet with Laban on the wages he should receive when he finally could leave—he would only take the speckled and spotted sheep and goats. When Laban agreed, Jacob devised an ingenious strategy amounting to what we would term genetic engineering today. By creating a highly conducive breeding environment for only the speckled and spotted among the flocks, Jacob managed to multiply them exponentially. (See Genesis 29–30.) It's baffling why the peeled rods he placed near the watering holes would send those rams into breeding overdrive but doing so clearly worked!

I was most impressed with Jacob's confidence throughout. Jacob was always shrewd and clever. If you recall, he outsmarted his older brother, Esau, and scammed his father into giving him the inheritance meant for the firstborn. However, Jacob's words to Rachel and Leah in Genesis 31:6–9 made it clear where the source of his confidence and trust lie: "With all my might I have served your father. Yet your father has deceived me and changed my wages ten times, but God did not allow him to hurt me.... *God has taken away the livestock of your father and given them to me*" (Gen. 31:6, 9, emphasis added). And further, in verse 12 the Angel of God spoke this to Jacob: "Lift your eyes…and see, *all* the rams…are streaked, speckled, and gray-spotted; *for I have seen all that Laban is doing to you*" (emphasis added).

Every time I read Genesis 31:12–13, I have to choke back my tears. Jacob had to endure twenty years of hardship in Laban's household. Yet God's eyes never departed from Jacob a fraction of a second throughout that time. Jacob was tenacious to the end and was triumphant when he finally departed from Laban's household.

My husband took his life on October 21, 2018. He suffered severely from depression for six months leading up to that day. Although we had worked closely together the past decade, building our real estate portfolio of properties in Frankfurt and Singapore, nothing prepared me for the tsunami of paperwork relating to legal and tax issues that awaited me after he died.

I had a simple strategy to keep me focused. Every single day, I adhered to and implemented the Lord's whisper in my ear: "Just keep moving. Keep it simple but keep it moving."

I have worked myself to the bone two years after his passing while shrouded in a cloud of trauma. The months of highly compressed, unrelenting tension seem surreal to me. Yet I simply focused on taking care of my kids and taking care of my business affairs.

I am not overstating it or being melodramatic when I say I have been through a lot. I was even scammed of literally hundreds of thousands of dollars in a severe lapse of business judgment a few months after my husband passed away. To be precise, I lost $450,000. It was an excruciating time. I felt as if my head were in a fog every day. I couldn't think clearly. I was in pain every waking minute. As fearful and acutely anxious as I was throughout those few months, I never stopped. I simply powered through whatever setback I faced. I kept telling myself that I had been through worse, and I could get through it because the Lord would get me through it. It's only money that's lost. In fact, the Lord gave me a powerful and effective strategy to call back in the spiritual realm the money that was lost.

Isaiah 45:3 says, "I will give you the treasures of darkness and hidden riches of secret places." It dawned on me that there is no such thing as lost money; it is out there somewhere in the world's economy, hidden or otherwise, and it was not beyond God's reach. The verse in Isaiah shows that God can bring it back to me from the secret places, even money that was ill-gotten or stolen from me. On top of that, the Bible mentions restitution of two, four, five, or even seven times what was stolen (Exod. 22:1, 7; Prov. 6:31; Luke 19:8).

For months, not only did I stand unwavering on Isaiah 45:3, but I also warred ferociously in my prayer closet against the enemy to call back my hidden riches from the secret places and to have them restored sevenfold, above and beyond what I lost. God gave me a further strategy to swim upstream, which I implemented quickly and consistently. I took the bold step of doubling down and sowing big financial seeds during those months. It paid off big-time. As I sowed, I saw my stock portfolio swelling by the day, and by the end of 2019, between my portfolio and the properties I sold, the Lord had recompensed me more than ten times the amount scammed from me.

Looking back, it was the Lord's strategy that focused and empowered me beyond ordinary human capacity. As I kept it simple and kept moving, no matter what I did—whether selling real estate, investing in stocks, or even managing the highly depressing and stressful probate process—I prospered. I have continually encountered uncommon favor at every turn. I pressed on my covenant with my Father as I pushed past every pain and bulldozed my way through trials. God has given me the strategy and tenacity to triumph over trials. Like Jacob in Genesis 31:12, I know He sees all that the enemy has done to me, and He is giving the livestock of the enemy to me on a silver platter.

Against all odds, I now find myself in a phenomenally better financial position than I ever was with my husband, something that would have been inconceivable on October 21, 2018. My God sees all that the enemy has done to me, and He always leads me in triumph in Christ Jesus. Always.

CHAPTER 3

Kings' Identity

You are a polymath king, not a jack-of-all-trades.

In June 2019 I published another article relating to kings. This is what I wrote in my article and continue to believe strongly:

Today, Jesus is on a search and rescue mission, to find kings who are in distress, hidden, lost or drowning in life and to gather them back to Himself. Why? He wouldn't hesitate to dash into abysmal darkness to rescue the one lost sheep. Similarly, He wouldn't hesitate to visit intimately with unsavory kings like Zacchaeus to transform [them].[1]

As I pointed out earlier, the clan of kings is like the missing tribe of Benjamin, nowhere to be found in the body of Christ. Yet Jesus is now on a massive hunt for that one lost sheep, that one lost tribe. We need to know what that sheep looks like, smells like, and sounds like. Knowing what kings are like is crucial. Once the clan is identified, legitimacy is then conferred by Christ Himself as the King of kings.

What Do Kings Look Like in the Natural?

Here are some prototypes of kings revealed to me by the Holy Spirit:

Polymath kings

Polymaths are highly intuitive. They are both specialists and generalists, thinking and operating at both micro and macro levels, solving problems creatively, and mastering technical and artistic fields with ease. For example, my late husband was not only a brilliant attorney but also an inventive cook who created recipes on the fly. I am a total geek when it comes to devouring voluminous knowledge about innovative tech or companies in the stock market. Blame it on the rigorous training of studying law. Flip a switch, and I am transformed from geek to interior décor artist, beautifying spaces, staging apartments for sale or rent.

Polymaths are always hungry to learn, continually questing for self-improvement. Their brains are constantly going at one hundred miles per millisecond. Some have multiple careers in a lifetime. Polymaths are often misunderstood or mistakenly labeled jacks-of-all-trades, but their true identity is more like a Renaissance man. Their ability to master different fields makes them great leaders. In fact, I believe that many people demonstrating attention deficit disorder symptoms, note symptoms not disorder, are polymaths in disguise. Recently I looked up the ADHD symptoms and saw that I could possibly relate to 80% of the symptoms, e.g., extreme impatience, talking over people (… occasionally!), misplacing things, not into details, results-focused, aggressive risk-taker etc. Early this month I thought I lost a $20,000 one carat diamond stud at the Hilton in Dallas. I almost became unhinged combing their lobby on my knees! But truth be told, I reject the ADHD diagnosis, even if the symptoms seem to linger. On the contrary, I choose to receive the redemption that God has in store for people with such symptoms -- I elect to view myself as a super high performer with exceptional ability to think through complexity, see things from new perspectives and accomplish multiple difficult tasks within short timelines. ADHD people are polymaths in disguise. Regardless of the world's labeling or diagnosis, *you* are a polymath king *created* by God.

Beast kings

There are kings who are like the beast in the story *Beauty and the Beast*. The modern-day beast prototype is a highly successful king who lives life buffered by his moat of wealth and power. He chooses to insulate himself with a select few due to a general distrust and disdain of people, built over the years by people's constant clamoring for money or favor from him. God doesn't feature much in the equation of his success journey. The way he sees it, he built his empire entirely by the work of his hands. He is powered by his own vows made early in life to overcome poverty and defeat, and he didn't see God in the mix as he climbed his way to the top. In fact, the beast king often feels abandoned by God, as if God has turned His back on him. Yet despite his success, the beast king experiences deep emotional isolation and disconnect because of his wariness of people at large. This is the total personification of that one lost sheep.

For his void to be filled, the beast king needs to encounter unconditional acceptance and grace—not judgment or condemnation—before his true identity as a benevolent king will emerge. Just as Zacchaeus, who was bound by greed and marginalized by his community, was changed by one encounter with Jesus in Luke 19, the beast king needs to encounter the true King, who will embrace him unconditionally and melt the crust around his heart.

> **The Son of Man has come to seek and to save that which was lost.**
>
> —LUKE 19:10

Nerd kings

In 2021, the Lord highlighted another prototype of kings that are literally everywhere, right under our noses. Powerful and prevailing, they dominate the pinnacle of every industry imaginable…introducing the nerd kings. You can be a tech nerd, an auto mechanic nerd to a baking nerd, highly skilled and possessing specific knowledge and skills that no one else does and that have propelled you to the top of your industry. The appetite of nerd kings for industry-specific knowledge, data, analysis, and detail is vociferous. They have exceptional memory for detail, sometimes bordering on trivia. Most of all, they possess an extraordinary ability to connect the dots to keep them ahead of the game. They are the visionaries, prophets, and titans of industry, Elon Musk being a glaring example of one. Even though he completed degrees in physics and economics, he tweeted on July 8, 2018, that he considers himself to be an engineer.[2] He is the epitome of a nerd king.

Closer to home, my buddy and Austin business partner Christopher B. Smith, a real estate business owner, investor, and realtor boss with a team of realtors working under him is a prime example of a nerd king. As a former leading tech executive, he can code and to make sense of massive data that most real estate people do not. He even developed an algorithm to search out properties that are the best fit for his clients' needs. Working with him has been a blessing beyond words. His talent for managing subcontractors, numbers, construction data, and plans is indispensable as we progress through our massive and complex flip project in Austin. Christopher is also a purebred polymath—he's an excellent gourmet cook to boot!

Diamond-in-the-rough kings

Other kings are like raw, uncut diamonds, like Saul and David, weighed down by carnality. They may fly off the handle on occasion, have road rage, or even cuss. Confession time: that's me behind the wheel!

When diamonds are mined and still in their uncut form, they could easily pass for crystal rock sugar, possessing little value—worthless. Only after a rigorous process of cutting, cleaving, sawing, bruting, and polishing does their nature as diamonds surface. Most believers are in this category, requiring cutting and polishing to manifest their kingly DNA, for their true potential to surface.

Innately every king—whether a polymath, beast, nerd, or diamond in the rough—has an uncommon determination to fight, to conquer, to succeed, to dominate, and to subdue. Left to their own devices and without God, they become narcissistic, causing collateral damage as they live selfishly and without purpose.

Therefore, before it is too late, kings must become aware of the legitimacy of their God-given birthright and inherent wiring to fight, conquer, and dominate. They must understand what they are here for, and they must be connected with the eternal purposes planted in their hearts by God. They must step into realization that they "are His workmanship, created in Christ Jesus for good works, which God prepared beforehand that [they] should walk in them" (Eph. 2:10).

And once kings come to grasp the fullness of who they are, they will step into and embrace the multifaceted roles of a king—that of a steward, a servant, and a priest.

Kings Are Stewards

A steward is a person entrusted with the duty of managing assets that belong to someone else—that is to say, the owner. You and I have an owner—God Himself. Kings are God's appointed stewards, created to manage God's assets well to advance God's kingdom and purposes on this earth.

Jesus once told the parable of the talents, in which servants, or stewards, were entrusted with some of their master's money while he was away on a journey. When the master returned, the stewards who had done well with the talents entrusted to them were commended with the words "Well done, good and faithful servant; you were faithful over a few things, I will make you ruler over many things" (Matt. 25:21). As believers we need to remember that when all is said and done and we meet Jesus face to face, we will want to hear Him say those words: "Well done, good and faithful servant."

You are not your own. You do not belong to yourself but to Jesus, who paid for your freedom through the cross.

> **Do you not know that…you are not your own? For you were bought at a price.**
>
> —1 CORINTHIANS 6:19–20

Everything that runs through your life and your fingers does not belong to you, be it your job, your employees, your property, your house, your tenants, all your possessions from cars and clothing to jewelry and junk, your bank accounts, your talents, your gifts, your ministry calling, your loved ones, your children, your relationships, or your spouse. It all belongs to God; you are His appointed steward. He has entrusted you with all the above to manage. But one thing does belong to you: the responsibility of stewardship. That is on you. The *responsibility* of stewardship is what you need to *own*. How you steward all that has been entrusted to you is on you!

I personally find *time* to be the hardest commodity to steward. Everyone has the same 24 hours a day, 7 days a week, 365 days a year, and 1 lifetime. We all have the same temptations of fear, procrastination, distraction, or inaction when we feel overwhelmed by difficult tasks. But the key is to push yourself to reach forward in pursuit of your calling, the way I have had to — for instance, in writing this book, it's taken two years. Part I was completed by end of 2020 and I was so exhausted I took a year's break and focused on investing activities. Part II was finally completed in June 2022. But the point is not to give up! At times, your energy level is higher, and you run faster and accomplish more. At times, you need to slow down, rest, and recharge so you don't burn out and give up altogether. You must effectively steward your time as you "press toward the goal to the prize of the high calling of God in Christ Jesus" (Phil. 3:14, MEV).

Not only are kings stewards, but I believe kings have to be master stewards, masterful at the art of stewarding. Here's a real-life instance of one: I saw a CNBC documentary on the history of Chick-fil-A. Chick-fil-A was the third-largest restaurant chain in the United States by sales in 2019, behind only Starbucks and McDonald's. Chick-fil-A was founded by Truett Cathy, who was known to have a strong Christian faith. It is widely known that Chick-fil-A is overtly living out Christian values and traditions in its business model, which is strange by industry standards, but its model has produced fantastic results and sales to the envy of competitors.[3] In the CNBC documentary there was a clip of a plaque stating Chick-fil-A's corporate purpose:

> **To glorify God by being a faithful steward of all that is entrusted to us. To have a positive influence on all who come in contact with Chick-fil-A.**[4]

I was stunned at the level of faithful stewardship when I first saw that plaque in the documentary clip. I aspire to reach that same level myself, to be a master steward king. I am nowhere near that, but I won't stop trying.

Here's a question for you: As you read this book and encounter the revelations I am sharing with you, how will you steward what you have learned? Will you respond or retreat? Will you respond to the king DNA deposited in you by diligently applying the principles in this book? Or will you retreat and leave this book to gather dust on a bookshelf cluttered with other Christian literature?

Remember, you are not your own. You do not belong to yourself but to Jesus, who paid for your freedom through the cross. Paul penned it beautifully in Galatians 2:20, one of my personal mottoes that keeps me going on down days:

> **I have been crucified with Christ; it is no longer I who live, but Christ lives in me.**

Kings Are Servants

Apart from the title of King of kings, Jesus is often referred to in the Bible as the Servant. The Gospel of Matthew also confirms that Jesus fulfilled an Old Testament prophecy referring to Him as a servant:

> **...that it might be fulfilled which was spoken by Isaiah the prophet, saying: "Behold! My Servant whom I have chosen, My Beloved in whom My soul is well pleased!"**
>
> —MATTHEW 12:17–18

Jesus Himself stated His mission in Mark 10:45 clearly:

> **For even the Son of Man did not come to be served, but to serve, and to give His life a ransom for many.**

The famous scene in John 13 where Jesus insisted to Peter on washing the disciples' feet demonstrates powerfully His heart of servanthood, even though He knew from the outset He was going to be betrayed that same evening by His own disciple Judas Iscariot (John 13:2). He washed all their feet, including Judas' feet. In this passage Jesus commanded His disciples, therefore including us, His believers today, to follow His example and serve as He did. His explanation in John 13:13–15 has become the bedrock of Christian servanthood and leadership in churches around the world and inspired countless books and sermons:

> **You call Me Teacher and Lord...so I am. If I then, your Lord and Teacher, have washed your feet, you also ought**

to wash one another's feet. For I have given you an example, that you should do as I have done to you.

The emphasis here is twofold: He serves, but He also leads, and He leads through serving the very people who are following Him. He is therefore commonly known as the Servant King, not just the Servant. As a king and leader, you are to follow His example as He commanded, to lead through service and to serve through leadership.

This concept of leadership through service is the total opposite of what leadership and ruling in the world looks like, which is typically through sheer domination of strong personalities and tyrannical imposition of their will. Jesus elaborated on this more clearly in Matthew 20:25–28, where He was rebuking the two brothers, Zebedee's sons, who were jostling for leadership positions under Him out of wrong motives. The Passion Translation hit the nail on the head with its version of Matthew 20:25–28. Jesus told His disciples:

> **Kings and those with great authority in this world rule oppressively over their subjects, like tyrants. But this is not your calling. You will lead by a completely different model. The greatest one among you will live as the one who is called to serve others, because the greatest honor and authority is reserved for the one with the heart of a servant. For even the Son of Man did not come expecting to be served by everyone, but to serve everyone, and to give His life in exchange for the salvation of many.**

This then brings us to the next question: How do we lead by service? It goes against the natural human instinct of leaders to dominate through the assertion of one's will. Just because He said we should do it doesn't mean we *can*. The key lies in His statement in John 13:15: "For I have given you an example, that you should do *as I have done to you*" (emphasis added).

As a king or leader, you can serve because He served you first. He washed the feet of the disciples first. He took care of you first. He gave His life for you first so that your sins were wiped away on a clean slate when you became a believer. He delivered healing and freedom to you first. You can serve because He *loved* you *first*. First John 4:16–19 (TLV) empowers us with the ability to serve and to love just as our Servant King, Jesus, does:

> **So we have come to know and trust in the love that God has for us....In this way, love is made perfect among us.... For just as He is, so also are we in this world....We love, because He first loved us.**

When you come to know, trust, and receive His love for you first, it is easy for you to serve others as He does and to lead as He does. Therein lies the key to emulating His heart. The heart of a servant is one that is overflowing with love and selflessness for people in general. The Servant King does not view His followers, including you and me, as inferior in any way, shape, or form. In fact, in John 15:13–15 Jesus took this even further and elevated His disciples from servants to friends:

> **Greater love has no one than this, than to lay down one's life for his friends. You are My friends....No longer do I call you servants...but I have called you friends.**

Learn to know, trust, and receive His unending, transformative love for you first. It's the key to being empowered and motivated to serve and lead just as He does. As I have been a recipient of so much of His love and healing, it has been easy for me to serve others this past decade. I can no longer recall how many times I have gone to street outreaches, laying hands on people (some homeless, some junkies) while giving them words of knowledge or praying for their physical healing or sharing the gospel spontaneously with people in my everyday life. This has ranged from the wife of a billionaire to my masseuse or workers renovating my properties. Or the time when I prayed for my Muslim real estate agent and his pregnant wife and laid hands on her baby bump. Just a few days before this writing in October 2020, I ministered to one of my home staff members, my personal chef, to receive Christ into her heart. She even got her back healed! That's not to mention the countless times I ministered to my own team members under my leadership, whether it was leading meetings at my home or organizing the Kings & Wealth conferences. Leading by serving, serving by leading—they go hand in hand, for just as He is, so are we.

Another critical trademark of Jesus our Servant King is His *humility*. No doubt, you are thinking again, "Easier said than done!" And that is true. I am not saying it's easy—but I am saying it's critical. Having humility is just about the most fundamental tenet of Christianity 101—"let each esteem others better than himself" (Phil. 2:4)—a trait that is counterintuitive to every human being on the planet. Philippians 2:5–8 (TLV) describes accurately the extent of Jesus' humility:

> **Have this attitude in yourselves, which also was in Messiah Yeshua, who, though existing in the form of God, did not consider being equal to God a thing to be grasped. But He emptied Himself—taking on the form of a slave, becoming the likeness of men and being found in appearance as a man. He humbled Himself—becoming obedient to the point of death, even death on a cross.**

Paul is pointing out to us the inconceivable extent to which Jesus, our Servant King, humbled Himself and that we believers need to have a similar attitude. It is particularly critical for kings to understand the significance of staying humble and grounded in the process of becoming and being kings. Let me use an example from my own life.

My late husband was one of the top attorneys in Germany in private equity law practice. His team was highly ranked over the years. Over four hundred people showed up at his funeral. The top partners at his firm flew in from London, New York, and Brussels. The firm transported busloads of attorneys in designer black suits to the church where a memorial was being held in his honor. Many millionaires and fund managers who were his clients came to convey their condolences about Mario's passing. I am accustomed to moving around high-net-worth individuals, most of whom are extremely brilliant, charming, kind, and generous and many of whom I like and have known for many years. But if I can pinpoint their number one flaw or sin, it is pride—their refusal to acknowledge the God factor in the equation for their success and abundance.

Four years ago I read a powerful book by a highly renowned author taking a deep dive into the spirit of Leviathan, a marine demon and ruling principality. According to him, Leviathan has a stranglehold on entire cities located near bodies of water, be it the coast or rivers or lakes. Leviathan manifests itself in the form of pride. In societies and places where Leviathan has a stranglehold, there is an unusually low rate of salvation. Yet there is often a concentration of wealth and prosperity in these societies.[5]

That struck a chord in me about the world's biggest cities, such as London, New York, and Hong Kong, where I lived and worked for almost seven years. They are all coastal cities with a high concentration of wealth and low rates of salvation. My city is also on the water. Frankfurt is officially called Frankfurt am Main, meaning Frankfurt on the Main (River). It is home to the European Central Bank (ECB), which governs monetary policy of the euro area and holds the keys to the wealth of the nineteen European Union (EU) nations that are part of the euro area. The ECB building is located right on the riverbank. There is much wealth in my region that is under the radar. Many millionaires and high-net-worth individuals virtually unknown to the world live in my city and the surrounding region. Sadly, I can think of only one or maybe two such individuals in my local circles who are sold out for Jesus.

There is a huge weight attached to stewarding wealth and power that most people are unaware of. There is an irresistible seduction that comes along with money flowing through your hands into your burgeoning bank accounts. That growing feeling of success is like a silky whisper in your ears telling you how great you are, and before you know it, you start attributing success to yourself, not God. That seductive lie creeps up on you surreptitiously. Before you realize it, the tentacles of pride have invaded every corner of your personality and being. I catch myself being seduced by that lie occasionally. I also saw my late husband falling for the lie oftentimes over the years as his career took off and we enjoyed phenomenal financial growth.

Everyone is vulnerable and susceptible to the same powerful lie. No one is immune to the sin of pride, which I believe was Lucifer's original sin.

God knows what is in man's heart. He forewarned us multiple times. Deuteronomy 8:7–18 lays out that age-old temptation as plain as day:

> For the LORD your God is bringing you into a good land, a land of brooks of water, of fountains and springs, that flow out of valleys and hills; a land of wheat and barley, of vines and fig trees and pomegranates, a land of olive oil and honey; a land in which you will eat bread without scarcity, in which you will lack nothing....When you have eaten and are full, then you shall bless the LORD your God for the good land which He has given you.

> Beware that you do not forget the LORD your God... lest—when you have eaten and are full, and have built beautiful houses and dwell in them; and when your herds and your flocks multiply, and your silver and your gold are multiplied, and all that you have is multiplied; when

> your heart is lifted up, and you forget the LORD your God
> who brought you out of the land of Egypt, from the house
> of bondage…then you say in your heart, "My power and
> the might of my hand have gained me this wealth." And
> you shall remember the LORD your God, for it is He who
> gives you power to get wealth.

The root sin of pride causes successful kings to become beast kings, a king prototype mentioned earlier in this chapter. The moat of wealth and power beast kings have built in their lives creates a false sense of security, as their trust and confidence are rooted in their riches and their status. They live only for themselves, have no sense of purpose in their relentless pursuit, and have no awareness of their true identities as kings that should be heralding God's kingdom on earth.

The focus here is not to encourage people to engage in spiritual battles against the Leviathan spirit. Many of us are not mandated for that battle or do not have the spiritual mantle to battle that level of principality. However, the antidote to pride, which the Lord revealed specifically to me, is to stay humble and to honor others. This will counter the spirit of Leviathan that rules many wealthy cities and principalities.

Proverbs 4:23 is a reminder that above all, you must "keep your heart with all diligence"—no matter how high your ascent is. Your portion is to follow in the footsteps of your King and manifest His Servant King DNA in your life. There is too much at risk not to do so. Genesis 4:7 (NIV) is another key warning as to how easily kings can fall prey to pride:

> Sin is crouching at your door; it desires to have you, but
> you must rule over it.

The enemy doesn't play fair. Pride will take you down swiftly, and it won't be long before greed and selfish ambition take over. Pride corrodes and erodes your true identity, if you let it. We are servant kings—leaders to serve, not expecting to be served—for the greatest honor and authority is reserved for the one with the heart of a servant.

> **If anyone serves Me, let him follow Me; and where I am, there My servant will be also. If anyone serves Me, him My Father will honor.**
>
> —JOHN 12:26

Kings Are Priests, While Priests Are Kings

As we look at this last aspect of the identity of kings, remember that kings are best described as leaders in varying fields, be that in business, arts, entertainment, industry, or government. Kings are positioned at the top of the leadership structure of a team, a department, an enterprise, or an institution.

As I was digging into the statistics of the general population, it came to light that you may face overwhelming odds stacked against you on your journey to become a king. Only 15.6 percent of the US population are entrepreneurs.[6] And for purposes of illustration, the statistics for women in my old profession rising through the ranks of leadership are dire. While more than 50 percent of graduating law students are women, only 19.6 percent of equity partners are women.[7] I was one of those women attorneys who never made it to equity partnership. There were many factors in play, but I gave up a decade of professional experience to create a home and support my husband through the phenomenal growth of his career.

Here's my point: kings are a special and rare breed in the general population. Yet God still called us, both His sons and His daughters, to become kings by rising to leadership in this world, outside church walls, to manifest His kingdom on earth. That is the strategic mandate of kings. God's sons and daughters must have the courage to defy overwhelming odds and overcome obstacles in their oftentimes lonesome journeys.

God chose us to defy the odds. God chose you to defy the odds. He handpicked you precisely because of your past, your brokenness, your quirks, your fears, and your obstacles, for those very same weaknesses can be turned into your strengths that will help you rule as a king.

Deuteronomy 7:6–9 is a powerful passage for kings. I highly recommend that you take the time to declare and proclaim the verses out loud multiple times. Proclaiming these verses over yourself can release a radical power to heal the brokenness in your core to make room for the king He placed in you to come forth boldly:

> For you are a holy people to the LORD your God; the LORD your God has chosen you to be a people for Himself, a special treasure above all the peoples on the face of the earth. The LORD did not set His love on you nor choose you because you were more in number than any other people, for you were the least of all peoples; but because the LORD loves you, and because He would keep the oath which He swore to your fathers, the LORD has brought you out with a mighty hand, and redeemed you.…Therefore know that the LORD your God, He is God, the faithful God who keeps covenant and mercy for a thousand generations with those who love Him and keep His commandments.

When I read this passage in light of the call to be kings, it was another of those pivotal aha moments where I burst into tears unexpectedly. He chose you to be His special treasure simply because He loves you—despite your failings or whatever inadequacies you think you might have. Not only that; He chose to exalt you to an even higher, dual calling—that of a king and a priest. Don't gloss over your calling. God made it clear:

[You] have made us kings and priests to our God; and we shall reign on the earth.

—REVELATION 5:10

Again, the Passion Translation gave poetic expression to this familiar verse:

But you are God's chosen treasure—priests who are kings, a spiritual "nation" set apart as God's devoted ones. He called you out of darkness to experience his marvelous light, and now he claims you as his very own. He did this so that you would broadcast his glorious wonders throughout the world.

—1 PETER 2:9, TPT

You are probably thinking, "I can barely wrap my head around being a king, much less a king and a priest. Why? How?"

You have a God who believes in you and has equipped you to achieve the impossible and to carry His glory to all corners of the world. It is all for His glory, so you get to brag on Him and not on you. You get to broadcast His glorious wonders throughout the world.

Let's examine a biblical model, and you will see that it is not as abstract as it sounds. King Hezekiah in 2 Chronicles is, for me, a prime example of a true king and priest. King Hezekiah understood his double anointing and mantle. When the nation of Israel was in crisis, he rose to the occasion to operate in the priestly capacity.

For there were many in the assembly who had not sanctified themselves.... For a multitude of the people... had not cleansed themselves, yet they ate the Passover contrary to what was written. But Hezekiah prayed for them, saying, "May the good LORD provide atonement for everyone who prepares his heart to seek God, the LORD God of his fathers, though he is not cleansed

> according to the purification of the sanctuary." And the
> LORD listened to Hezekiah and healed the people.
>
> —2 CHRONICLES 30:17–20

It sounds as if Israel and Judah found themselves in a hot mess, to the point that "the priests and the Levites were ashamed" (2 Chron. 30:15). Clearly the priests and the Levites were not doing their duty of asking God for atonement for the people, and still others were eating the Passover uncleansed. These were unpardonable, grave violations of the Torah.

King Hezekiah saw the need of his people and the void left by the priests. He had compassion for his people, just as Christ had for the masses He ministered to. Without hesitation Hezekiah stepped in to fill the leadership vacuum left by the priests and to intercede powerfully for his people for an atonement they clearly didn't deserve. In the absence of atonement, the people were as good as toast. God was moved by Hezekiah's powerful and effective appeal. He answered Hezekiah's prayer and promptly healed the nation.

A king who can wear the hat of a priest demonstrates how a king can be in tune with God's heart. A king is naturally invested in his people because they are his subjects, under his rule and dominion. If his people are in trouble, it goes without saying that their king must step in to help in some way, shape, or form. Further, a king who can also function as a priest has empathy for his people and insight into their plight. I believe that if a leader can step up not only to rule and govern but also to stand as mediating priest for his people, there are double, triple, quadruple, or even unquantifiable blessings laid up for the king and his people.

Can you imagine the potential if kings today were to function as priests to their people? Or if CEOs were to pray for their enterprises and their employees instead of sweeping things under the carpet and sending them to human resources? Or if politicians were to pray for their constituents?

In 2020, no one was able to quantify the losses as millions of businesses and families fought for economic survival. What if President Trump had set aside thirty minutes a day and get on his face in the Oval Office to pour his heart out before God, to ask Him to heal the land? Since Germany has a primary leadership role in the EU, what if the then Chancellor Angela Merkel had interceded earnestly before God on behalf of the 440 million-plus people in the twenty-seven member states? Wouldn't it be infinitely powerful if they had given God the helm of leadership in their governing of almost 700 million lives? Can you even begin to imagine the power and healing that could have been unleashed if they had operated as priests for their nations as well? The same questions can be posed for President Biden or the current German Chancellor Olaf Scholz.

I am a king and a priest. A king is who I am. So is being a priest. I cannot separate the duality of my mantle. It's like two sides of a coin. I engage in business ministry and Christian ministry. If I focus on only one type of ministry, I start feeling as if I am out of whack and I get bored out of my mind. This duality is how God wired me. I need to be conquering outside the temple and participate in building the temple. However, as I am a king, I have resources available to me unlike most priests or other ministers, who rely on external sources of financial support. For the past decade, I have been able to self-finance all my ministry activities thus far, from hosting my spiritual parents in Frankfurt, to holding Kings and Wealth Conferences in top locations such as the five-star Jumeirah Frankfurt hotel with meals included, to flying to Kenya for a weeklong teaching engagement with my ministry assistant in tow, to renting double-sized booths at the Frankfurt New Age convention for evangelistic outreaches to pray for people. If not for wanting to give people the opportunity to sow, I literally have no need for fundraising. Do you realize how much freedom and peace that is for a minister?

As I started walking out both kingly and priestly functions, the Lord confirmed my journey as a king and a priest by drawing people wearing this dual mantle. My co-teacher at the 2019 Kings and Wealth Conference was Kevin W. Crystal. He is a fellow king and priest. He is a council member in his city, he has his day job in commercial real estate, and he is an investor as well. Simultaneously he is remarkably strong in teaching the Word and is an evangelist-preacher specializing in prison ministry. Many inmates have given their lives to the Lord through his prison ministry. As a king and a priest, he is guided by God's wisdom and prayerful counsel when he is operating in the realm of government. Having government officials who understand priesthood and pray for their cities and constituents will bring lasting change and immeasurable blessing and favor, as well as alignment with divine purposes.

Another good friend of mine, Cris Zimmermann, is the amazing visionary founder of an evangelistic ministry called Kirche in Aktion (Church in Action), a ministry best described as expansionary and entrepreneurial in spirit, sending out what he terms *urban missionaries* in our region and truly embodying the spirit of *ekklesia*. When I got more acquainted with Cris, I was pleasantly surprised to find that he is one of the sharpest and most successful real estate investors I know. Like me, he can finance kingdom activities pretty much by himself, if he wants to. He has tremendous resources available to him. He has a huge understanding of tapping into a reservoir of unlimited kingdom wealth and resources at his disposal for kingdom purposes. This is a total game changer on so many levels—imagine never having to beg, plead or cajole others to fundraise for your ministry activities!

One final observation regarding kings who are priests: due to the duality of the mantle, priestly kings are wired to get results, whether they operate as kings or priests. Therefore, kings who are also priests are unstoppable.

If you are a pastor or vocational minister who has gotten hold of this book, I have a word from the Lord specifically for you. You might be wearing the priestly mantle, and you might be wearing it well. You might be an anointed preacher, a beloved pastor of your congregation, or even a commissioned apostle or prophet. I am not taking anything away from that. You are the Lord's anointed in your area of authority and spiritual gifting, and I have no authority to touch that.

However, if you are reading this book, please know that you are also called to be a king. You are part of a *royal* priesthood:

> **But you are a chosen generation, a royal priesthood, a holy nation, His own special people, that you may proclaim the praises of Him who called you out of darkness into His marvelous light.**
>
> —1 PETER 2:9

In Revelation 1:5–6 John wrote, "To Him who loved us and washed us from our sins in His own blood, and has made us kings *and* priests…" (emphasis added). This is reinforced in Revelation 5:10, where John wrote, "[You] have made us kings *and* priests to our God; and we shall reign on the earth" (emphasis added).

You are not one or the other; you are both.

You do not get to pass the buck to members of your congregation and leave the creation of provision to them by pressing them to tithe or give offerings, all the while ignoring your mantle of kingship. You have the responsibility and ability to also succeed in worldly spheres because you too have inherited the DNA of a king and are created to flourish as one. You were created to rule and to create wealth—because you are a priest *and* a king.

Imagine enjoying alternative streams of revenue and being independent of church-based income. Imagine not having to beg, plead, or cajole others for money. What would your world look like with that kind of freedom?

Priests, you need to stop dodging that crown thrown at you by Jesus. It's a crown, not a grenade, and it's *your* crown to wear. It's time to stop dodging, hesitating, and retreating. Pick up your crown and dust off the dirt. Step into your appointed sphere of ruling. Take that slice of territory carved out for you by God before the foundation of the world.

The New Mindsets for Taking Territory

Kings will not stop until they recover all. Kings are all out to win. #kingsunstoppable

God-mandated kings are unstoppable. By *unstoppable*, I am referring to the way we are wired—metaphorically speaking, we are God's yeast.

Jesus compared the kingdom of heaven to yeast in Matthew 13:33, saying that yeast never stops spreading until it permeates every part of the dough. As yeast, you and I are God's stealth weapons, wired to expand God's kingdom until it infiltrates, permeates, and dominates every part of society. To paraphrase, it is simply the destiny of kings and their lifelong function and assignment to take territory for God—a never-ending quest for which they are wired.

King David personified this kingly function of taking territory for God to the hilt. David was a warrior king with incredible insights to secure victories. He not only battled the Philistines but crushed them resoundingly, and he also wrested control of the key city of

Jerusalem away from the Jebusites. When I visited Israel in 2018, I was astounded by how David built and fortified the city of David in the middle of Jerusalem three thousand years ago. The city of David was also the royal residence during his reign. King David built the city of David on a ridge surrounded by valleys, thereby camouflaging the city of David from the enemy's view. It was situated high enough to give David and his army a vantage point from which to spot any oncoming attacks from enemies early. David was therefore able to secure the city of Jerusalem, and he turned Jerusalem into Israel's political and religious center. With Jerusalem as his base camp, he was able to conquer and annex the coastal region and many small kingdoms. King David succeeded eventually in unifying the whole of Israel.

What kind of mindsets make it possible for people such as King David to succeed? The Holy Spirit has given me a few clues, and I can't wait to share them with you!

Let's examine a few mindsets that I believe are paramount and must be adopted before the lifetime quest of taking territory can be accomplished.

Strategy-Seeking Mindset—Inquire of the Lord First

Not only is this mindset key, but it is the foundation for all the other mindsets. You must inquire of the Lord first and seek His strategy to succeed as a king. David constantly sought God's counsel and strategy before going into battle. First Samuel 13:14 and Acts 13:22 call David a man after God's own heart, referring to David's intimate relationship with God, a closeness that developed from the time he was a teenager shepherding his father's flocks alone in the fields. This closeness undergirded everything David did and was the key to his successful reign.

David's interaction with the Lord in 1 Samuel 30 demonstrates this closeness, along with David's humility in always deferring to the Lord's will first. It also demonstrates his incredible willingness and obedience to execute God's instructions without hesitation once he got them.

> **So David inquired of the LORD, saying, "Shall I pursue this troop? Shall I overtake them?"**
>
> **And He answered him, "Pursue, for you shall surely overtake them and without fail recover all."**
>
> **So David went.**
>
> —1 SAMUEL 30:8–9

And in case you're wondering how that story ended, David recovered all, just as the Lord said (1 Sam. 30:18–20).

In 2 Samuel 5:23–24 the Lord detailed to David a strategy that was coupled with minute-by-minute, blow-by-blow directions, to defeat the Philistines:

> **Therefore David inquired of the LORD, and He said, "You shall not go up; circle around behind them, and come upon them in front of the mulberry trees. And it shall be, when you hear the sound of marching in the tops of the mulberry trees, then you shall advance quickly. For then the LORD will go out before you to strike the camp of the Philistines."**

I was stunned by this level of specificity. In the past, all battle scenes and strategies recounted in Scripture went right over my head. But recently, what the Lord revealed to David caught my eye and made complete sense to me for the first time. To ensure victory, the Lord told David how to ambush the Philistines by utilizing the element of surprise. God's plan for David to ambush the Philistines would have put the fans of Sun Tzu's *The Art of War* to shame!

David had no qualms about always inquiring of the Lord first, even though as monarch of the kingdom, David had teams of counsel and prophets at his disposal. Yet God remained David's constant and foremost go-to. This was because David knew God had his back in every battle. His trust and intimacy with God were developed over decades, in the fields and in the caves.

Hence, staying close to the Lord and seeking His will is paramount for a king. There is no substitute for strategy and counsel released from the throne of God. After all, the core function and assignment of kings is to execute heaven's plans on earth!

Forceful Mindset—The Violent Take It by Force

In Matthew 13:33, when Jesus compared the kingdom to yeast, which multiplies until it fills the loaf entirely, He was reiterating Genesis 1:28, the core mandate, function, and assignment of kings:

> **Be fruitful and multiply; fill the earth and subdue it; have dominion over...every living thing that moves on the earth.**

Recall that the original Hebrew word for *subdue* is *kabash*, a word that conjures up imagery of violence and force. The imagery of violence conjured up by the word *kabash* brings to my remembrance what Jesus said in Matthew 11:12:

> **The kingdom of heaven suffers violence, and the violent take it by force.**

Matthew 11:12 is one of those head-scratching verses that make you go, "Huh?" when you read it for the first time. It only finally clicked when I read that verse together with Matthew 13:33 and Genesis 1:28.

Not only do Genesis 1:28 and Matthew 13:33 interpret and illuminate Matthew 11:12, but suddenly what Jesus said takes on life with the power of a command. I see Jesus commanding us to take back and recover territory lost to the enemy for *thousands of years, since the fall of man*, and to restore God's original plan on earth.

But for this plan to come to fruition, there is no getting around this—it must be done by *force*.

Let me qualify that I am not talking about resorting to physical force or violence. Second Corinthians makes that abundantly clear:

> **For though we walk in the flesh, we do not war according to the flesh. For the weapons of our warfare are not carnal but mighty in God for pulling down strongholds, casting down arguments and every high thing that exalts itself against the knowledge of God, bringing every thought into captivity to the obedience of Christ.**
>
> —2 CORINTHIANS 10:3–5

Nevertheless, it is war.

No longer are you and I to live a life of passivity in the guise of religious submissiveness. Kings are to *subdue*, not submit. No longer should we submit to the lies of the enemy and let him walk all over us, resulting in powerless lives deficient in kingdom advancement.

For the kingdom to advance and permeate through every part of society, kings must have the mentality of a holy violence. The kingdom can be advanced only if kings do not fear taking society back from the grasp of the enemy. Kings must assert and exert God's power and influence society. This connects with my second launch-pad vision, in which I saw continuous warring and the bloodshed of kings on the battlefield. The kingdom of heaven can advance only when kings take back what the enemy stole—leadership of planet earth, influence over society. Kings must possess a *forceful mindset* to that end.

Winning Mindset—No Apologies, No Shame!

In Matthew 13:33 Jesus painted the picture of the yeast spreading throughout the entire dough. That is total domination at its best. In the parable of the mustard seed, which He told just before,

He likened the kingdom of heaven to the smallest of seeds that becomes the largest tree in the garden (Matt. 13:31–32).

Based on these two illustrations alone, Jesus was clearly not even remotely reticent about growth and domination to become the numero uno. It is His explicit plan for the kingdom of heaven, and His mandate to us is to accomplish that on His behalf. When He said He is the Alpha (Rev. 1:8), He meant He is the Alpha of all alphas in the whole universe. Therefore, I seriously doubt that His intention is for us to be betas. We are made to be alphas in His image.

To subdue and to dominate, you must battle, and you must win. You must have the will and mindset to win. You do not need to apologize for wanting to win. There is no shame in winning.

David was a warring king. We know that. But he was also a king who went all out to win. As I was watching *The Last Dance*, there was one line that Michael Jordan said in Episode 7 that stuck with me, "My mentality was to go out and win at any cost."

To be fair, these words might sound jarring to our religious ears, stuffed with false humility wax, but I dare you to find me the verse in the Bible that says David was embarrassed because he won and apologized for winning the battles. Truth be told, he was the total opposite of being apologetic or embarrassed by the act of winning. First Samuel 30 states twice that "David recovered all."

Then David attacked them *from twilight until the evening of the next day.* **Not a man of them escaped, except four hundred young men who rode on camels and fled. So David** *recovered all* **that the Amalekites had carried away, and David rescued his two wives. And nothing of theirs was lacking, either small or great, sons or daughters, spoil or anything which they had taken from them;** *David recovered all.* **Then David took all the flocks and herds they had driven before those other livestock, and said, "This is David's spoil."**

—1 SAMUEL 30:17–20, EMPHASIS ADDED

David was out to win! He clearly had no qualms in obliterating the enemy and returning with a resounding victory. David's winning attitude was no different from that of Michael Jordan, the basketball legend. David was a warring king, and he was determined to win at any cost.

There was another detail hidden in this passage that I never noticed before, up until recently while I was updating my materials. For the first time, I noticed it was documented, "David attacked them from twilight until the evening of the next day." That is a full twenty-four hours. When this detail became uncovered, it was as if scales came off my eyes. David attacked and attacked and attacked, and he didn't stop until he annihilated the enemy and recovered all that were taken by the enemy, including his two wives. Most men would have been contented with rescuing one of two wives LOL, but not David! He was intent on recovering all that was his. The phrase, 'he recovered all', was repeated for emphasis, because the Holy Spirit knew this detail might have gone over our heads. David took back everything that was taken from him by the enemy, no exception, no mercy. That was David's MO, modus operandi.

Further, to win, you need to get results. Kings are validated by results, and there is no shame in wanting to get results. This might seem obvious, but the truth is that people in the body of Christ are afraid of appearing to go for results, whereas outside of church and in the workplace, there is simply no question about that requirement. You are hired to perform and get results. You will be fired if you do not perform and get results. Why then do we insist on having different standards and mindsets at work and at church?

When I think of the titans of industry, I don't ever recall Elon Musk or Amazon CEO Jeff Bezos apologizing for their ambitions to dominate their industries. Tesla dominates the electric vehicle space, has the leading market share worldwide, and continues to expand its lead over other automakers in the field. Do you see Elon Musk acting coy about their dominance in the EV space? Occasionally he might let loose a statement (an example on May 1, 2020) that seems incongruent with the interests of the company he's leading, like the share price of Tesla is too high,[1] but you will never hear him say, let's give the competitors a chance at playing catch up. Similarly, do you see Jeff Bezos apologizing or being embarrassed by the outrageous success of Amazon? I don't think so.

David didn't apologize for winning. He took all that belonged to him. He recovered all. And he didn't stop until he recovered all. He was all out to win. Yet God didn't judge David to be ruthless or unscrupulous. After all, God found David to be a man after His own heart, who would do all His will (Acts 13:22). God's will for His kings today is, and remains to be, recovery and total domination of the planet.

What Happens When You Have the New Mindset

I have a ton of testimonies where I have personally deployed the mindset lessons detailed previously. Allow me to share just two with you.

Around 2008, my late husband joined his firm as cohead. He was very disgruntled with his cohead position, as he was promised sole leadership shortly after he joined. The promised promotion didn't happen. For a variety of reasons, he came home angry and frustrated every day from engaging in full-on office feuds. I remember trying to comfort him with religious textbook advice (which, to be fair, wasn't wrong in itself)—perhaps God felt he wasn't ready to take on the full reins of leadership. To his chagrin, this was confirmed by his bosses in the head office in New York. They told him bluntly that he lacked the maturity needed for the top job, even though he was responsible for bringing in the most revenue and was indisputably one of the best in his field. We didn't give up. I continued to intercede regularly for him and asked the Lord to keep prepping him for promotion.

It then came to a pivotal point where I sensed in my spirit the winds were shifting. If you put a gun to my head today, I can't for the life of me articulate what exactly it was. I told him about the shift I sensed, and I asked him to read the Book of Joshua. Stereotypical of a king, he literally commanded me (yes, he did!) to read it for him and give him an executive summary with bullet points. I countered, "Honey, I can't do this for you! You must read the book yourself! The Holy Spirit will give you a take that's going to be completely different from mine." He resisted initially but finally found the time to read it. He came back with something that totally blew my mind, something I never saw before.

In his typical abundant-words-are-an-abundant-waste-of-time manner, he said succinctly he was impressed with how Joshua united and consolidated the different tribes of Israel. I recall telling him, "Huh? That was in there the whole time?" I may have read the Bible much more than he did, but I never saw that in that chapter! It was God's unique takeaway for him. He heard clearly and executed the strategy right away with precision and focus. He went around his office and spoke with his team and staff about how he was going to rally the office together if he took over full management. (It was not a secret that the two top dogs were feuding.) He then communicated his strategy of unity and consolidation with his bosses in New York. Suddenly he was invited to fly to the head office together with his rival for a series of leadership meetings. The other partner was promptly fired in New York, and Mario was promoted to full leadership as sole managing partner in Germany for a few years until his buddy Georg Linde joined him at the helm to co-lead the German operations. The office catapulted to legal stardom under their leadership. They continue to be top ranked today in the legal industry. This was my husband's legacy that was established only because of the strategy God revealed to him personally. My husband sought strategy from the Lord, he executed what was revealed to him, and he won the territory that God meant for him to rule over.

As for me, I spent the whole of 2019 and 2020 personally administering his estate he passed. It is a full-time job, but instead of hiring outsiders, I decided to do the job myself. I didn't have the luxury of distinguishing between weekdays or weekends, night or day. I just worked nonstop.

One of my biggest challenges in administering the estate was how to raise cash to pay for the exorbitant estate taxes in Germany. In our years of marriage, we amassed a collective net worth that exposed us to almost 30 percent estate taxes on everything my husband owned. I consulted a real estate agent friend on this issue, saying that I was intending to sell some properties to raise the necessary cash to pay the German government. Our home was also, truthfully, too much house for my two sons and me. He agreed and advised that I consider listing my house sooner than later. I struggled with his counsel to put the house up for sale only one year after my husband's passing, not to mention the work that came along with vacating a house chock-full of furniture collected over seventeen years of marriage. The idea was just too daunting at that time. He then said I only needed to find the one buyer God had prepared for me. I believe the Lord used this brother to relay a strategy I needed at that time.

Heeding my friend's further advice, I did something that was critical. I asked the Lord specifically for a number to price the property. The Holy Spirit promptly gave me a number that was 30 percent above what my German real estate agent estimated as the fair market price. That number took the property into a whole different price category, posing new challenges, even though the Frankfurt market was at its peak and red-hot in the fall of 2019. My agent resisted when I said I wanted to reprice my property at the number the Holy Spirit gave me. I then told him point-blank on the phone that God said I would get my price. I stood my ground and refused to back down. At that moment, it didn't matter to me whether he believed in God. I needed to execute what I heard from God. Pronto. There was silence on the other end of the line. He then said these three words: "Ich glaub dir," meaning "I believe you." I listed the house off-market in October, bearing in mind that fall is usually a difficult time for selling houses.

I had a full-price offer in less than two weeks. I gave my real estate agent strength with my resolute faith, and to fight for my full asking price. I sold my house at €4.2 million, which was equivalent to US$4.7 million at that time. A blistering new record of €15,000 (US$17,000) per square meter was set for my district. My neighborhood, called Diplomats' Quarter, was already well-known for having the priciest real estate in the city, and I managed to set a record in my neighborhood.

There were other aspects that marked the hand of God throughout: I got the house under contract in late November 2019, just before COVID-19 news broke in January 2020. Amid the pandemic lockdown chaos in April 2020, I was battling the family court in Frankfurt to approve the sale for closing and funding. Around that time, the new owners suddenly expressed reservations that the house was overpriced but mentioned they didn't intend to abort the sale. Thankfully, shortly after, I got the court's approval, and the transaction closed without a hitch at the end of May 2020.

In the months leading up to May 2020, however, it became apparent that the family with two young children was perfect for the house. Had I waited to sell, I may have missed out on this perfect buyer that God had intended for me.

To recap, I turned to the Lord for strategy. Once I heard from God, I moved and executed the strategy without hesitation nor delay. I pushed to *win* and fought for the top price God gave me—no apologies, no shame. Just as my late husband did, I won and took territory for God. I am building a legacy for our family. No apologies needed!

I believe these victories in my life are only the beginning:

Your descendants shall possess the gate of their enemies.

—Genesis 22:17

CHAPTER 5

The New Standards for Taking Territory

Keep tweaking until you hit execution perfection. There is a process to success.

We have covered extensively mindsets that operate as a foundational framework to equip kings to take territory for God. To take territory effectively, it is paramount that kings win, specifically in their respective fields of calling. In other words, they must continually aim to become the *best in class* so that they get to bring home the trophy, or, in Old Testament lingo, the spoils!

An age-old topic covered by innumerable self-help books is how to win in life. Most people succeed in changing their mindsets by repeating mantras, dialing into positive thinking, using sheer determination, or having an "insane work ethic," as my former business coach, JT Foxx, likes to say (the latter two being enviable traits that I personally subscribe to). But as sons and daughters of the Most High, kings are called to build their lives on the cornerstone of Christ, the Word Himself. So, friends, let's win God's way. Let's declutter our souls and get our foundations right by renewing our minds through the filter of the Word.

The Solomon Gold Standard—Wisdom

Let's take a fresh look at a familiar passage:

> At Gibeon the LORD appeared to Solomon in a dream by night; and God said, "Ask! What shall I give you?"
>
> And Solomon said: "...Now, O LORD my God, You have made Your servant king instead of my father David, but I am a little child; I do not know how to go out or come in. And your servant is in the midst of Your people whom You have chosen, a great people, too numerous to be numbered or counted. Therefore give to Your servant an understanding heart to judge Your people, that I may discern between good and evil...."
>
> The speech pleased the Lord, that Solomon had asked this thing. Then God said to him: "Because you have asked this thing, and have not asked long life for yourself, nor have asked riches for yourself, nor have asked the life of your enemies, but have asked for yourself understanding to discern justice, behold, I have done according to your words; see, I have given you a wise and understanding heart, so that there has not been anyone like you before you, nor shall any like you arise after you."
>
> —1 KINGS 3:5–12

Wisdom is the gateway to a successful, abundant life. In fact, in verses 13 and 14 of the same passage, God was so pleased with Solomon's request for wisdom that He added riches, honor, and length of life. My firm belief is that walking in godly wisdom will result in all these other blessings that God imparted to Solomon being added to you over time.

Self-education or investing in acquiring new certifications in your chosen field is key to promotion. You must aim to *establish* yourself as the *best in class* or at the very least, an *expert* in your field. For that, you must beef up on your knowledge and expertise.

Successful people read a lot. Legendary investor Warren Buffett spends five to six hours per day reading newspapers and corporate reports.[1] Microsoft founder Bill Gates reads about fifty books per year.[2] There is also the famous "5-Hour Rule" written about widely by Michael Simmons.[3] Regardless of how full their schedules are, successful people always manage to find time to read or learn, whether it is an hour a day or five hours a week.

One key word of wisdom is from Warren Buffett, who is currently the sixth-wealthiest person in the world, with a net worth of $114 billion as of June 2022, as listed in Investopedia.[4] He has often been quoted as saying, to invest in oneself is the best thing that one can do. I couldn't agree more. The irony with Warren Buffett is this: he has been quoted a few times in the press mentioning that he regards Jeff Bezos as one of the best business minds of our time and he's missed the boat for not buying Amazon in its early years. Clearly with his age (he's ninety this year), he struggled with understanding the technology or the business model in the early years of Amazon and chose to stay on the sidelines. Buffet's strategy to invest only in companies whose business he understands reveals that everyone, including Buffet, faces the challenge of continual learning and self-education.

Nevertheless, it is precisely self-education that brought quantum leaps into my life, including monetizing my passions. When my kids were very young, I spent hours studying the Bible and listening to sermons on CDs. Yes, it's that long ago and it took that many years! I can't recall how many courses relating to Bible teaching, prophetic skills, or Christian leadership I have taken this past decade. I was also officially commissioned as a minister of the gospel in January 2017 with TRIBE Network, founded by my spiritual dad, Apostle Ryan LeStrange.

Since I am generally a quick study, I also taught myself real estate investing by watching HGTV and reading books. Yes, it's confession time—again! I am an unabashed reality-TV junkie. I learned how to remodel properties by watching Christina and Tarek on the HGTV show *Flip or Flop*.

Additionally, in 2016, I taught myself how to invest in the stock market, another passion that I have been able to monetize. In my previous life as an attorney, in which I had to review and reduce mountains of documentation into key points, I speed-read with ease. This skill comes in handy when it comes to monitoring the markets for my stock portfolio. It also helps that I am a compulsive reader. I haven't been keeping an actual count, but I would guesstimate that I read about ten to twenty articles and fifty headlines a day relating to corporate news and economic data. In my initial years of stock market investing, my kids were little, and I used to juggle chores or prepare meals while watching CNBC or Bloomberg in my kitchen. As much as I adore my boys, my brain was turning into mush while doing only plain vanilla mom chores. Ingesting and analyzing fundamentals of companies and monetizing that knowledge was like steroids for my brain.

One final testimony—the learning never stops. I am always on the lookout to learn from others. In 2020, I entered an exclusive network with high-net-worth investors and successful entrepreneurs by paying a fee of $5,000. That is chump change relative to the plethora of investment opportunities that I suddenly found myself in. I thought I was fast, but the pace in that network was so rapid that I could barely catch my breath in processing the deals and information thrown at me at the speed of sound. I learned that every interaction with a high-net-worth individual is chock-full of life lessons. At my least expected moment, God placed me on an accelerated growth trajectory through this network founded by my former business coach JT Foxx. Through him, I am beyond thankful to be connected with his brilliant tax advisor Charles Dombek, who has since become a pivotal figure in my wealth-building journey. Looking back, I can see how much I have grown as a global investor since. Yet it all started with my continual hunger to invest in learning from others who have gone further down the path of success than I have.

More importantly, I suddenly realized God was paving the way for me to connect with brilliant kings, beast or not, in the secular arena, something I never would have dreamed about when I began this journey to call out kings.

The Daniel Gold Standard—Excellence

Daniel 6:3 says:

> **Daniel distinguished himself above the governors and satraps, because an excellent spirit was in him; and the king gave thought to setting him over the whole realm.**

Oftentimes we use the word *excellence* so much that it starts to sound cliché, and we stop hearing it altogether. However, excellence is foundational to succeeding. Let me be more precise. It is not just a vague notion of being excellent—it's about *excellence in execution.*

When you have the vision, you need to execute the vision. Many of us in the body of Christ are wildly in love with the idea of having a vision, receiving a vision from the Lord, casting the vision, and so on. All the talk about vision is infinitely useless without any follow-through.

Plan.

An instrumental part of the follow-through process—planning— is considered by some as nonspiritual. Nothing could be further from the truth. The Holy Spirit loves detailed planning as much as big visions. He is equally involved in my big dramatic launchpad visions that started the Kings and Wealth journey as in the minute structuring and crafting of the words in this very book.

Confessional on planning: this is an area where I still have plenty of room to grow. I am a ballpark planner. Does that make sense? I am always looking ahead to where I want to be in a few years and setting the execution in motion. But I never plan right down to the smallest details. When I have an approximate plan in place with 80 percent of the details, I run with it and wing it along the way with the Holy Spirit. I then adjust my plan at every juncture if something unexpected or adverse pops up—or, to paraphrase, I *pivot*.

When you tend to do detailed planning and are a stickler for details, you are likely to be a good manager. I have been told often I am a visionary, which apparently means I am not as concerned with details as a manager would be. But regardless, I always achieve executing the vision and bringing it across the finish line, generally with outstanding results (wink, wink). No matter what comes, I will get it done. For a leader like me, it makes total sense to hire a process-oriented manager to assist in implementing my vision for a venture, whether it's an investment deal or a ministry conference. A good manager is vital in helping me achieve my goals.

You must plan to succeed. Don't drift. Without a plan, drifting is bound to happen since you will be waiting for something to happen instead of making things happen. The Holy Spirit presents us with a lot more opportunities than we are aware of. Once you have your strategy from the Lord, stop waiting on Him—He's waiting on you. You must execute swiftly when you have a plan in place. For example, my architect and I took six months to plan for the rebuilding of my 1938 house. We were able to plan down to the minutest detail. The construction itself was then completed in merely six months. That is considered phenomenal, record time by German construction standards for a full gut renovation.

You must plan to succeed. If you want to move up the ladder in your workplace, you must have a plan. Be proactive. Seek the Lord for strategy and create your own road map for promotion within your company or organization. If you have been working there for several months and have no intention of leaving, then you should be able to identify the promotion you desire. Before your next performance review, be ready to tell your bosses which position you are gunning for and have a plan mapping out clearly how you intend to get there and what you plan to do when you get to that position. This is how my late husband got the top job managing the firm, as I shared earlier. Instead of expecting to be on the defensive at the next review, as most people are, surprise your bosses by being on the offensive. Take your strategy from the Lord and run with it. But of course, watch your tone, honor your bosses, be highly appreciative, and focus on how you can help move the company's vision forward. Watch and marvel at how God will go ahead of you and have the doors swing wide open in your favor. This is how you are primed for promotion.

Execute.

Once you have a plan in place, it is time to move on to excellence in execution. Let me begin by using our cornerstone as an illustration.

Jesus—our Prophet, King, and Priest—is the epitome of excellence in execution, or, in His case, perfection in execution. It took Jesus only three years to accomplish everything He was supposed to, and He did it all perfectly. I am not sure if you realize this, but He had a choice. Free will was created by Him. He could have veered off anytime if He wanted to or simply given up and commanded millions of angels to take Him home to heaven, which they would have done in an instant. But He didn't. He was subject to every temptation known to mankind, and yet He was focused and uncompromising in His mission to be the perfect sacrifice for the sin of humanity. Not only did He get the job done, but He also managed to upend the course of humanity in the short time He walked the earth. Jesus Christ was the all-time eternal disruptor of heaven, earth, and hell. Jesus was relentless and perfect in executing His mission of eternal disruption. Friends, this is the role model that we have as a point of reference.

And as I have mentioned multiple times, we have His DNA. This means we have also inherited His DNA of excellence in execution. It's in there somewhere inside you, and it will manifest when you walk in focused obedience and in tandem with His Spirit.

Tweak.

Recently I shared this spontaneously on a Facebook Live, and it resonated with many viewers: *there is a process to success*. What I meant to say is it takes time; it takes investing in a learning curve to excel at something or anything. The secret is to tweak—to keep making any needed adjustments—until you nail it, until you hit execution excellence, or even perfection. The principle is that simple, but there is a learning curve involved. There is a process.

Start with baby steps. Practice tweaking your execution of the most ordinary things in life. Start with an ordinary task, such as making the perfect omelet. For me the ordinary tasks that needed some excellence in execution were making Chinese poached eggs and reverse parking. And just the other day, I finally achieved execution excellence in these two simple tasks.

First off, I managed to make the perfect Chinese poached eggs! I finally nailed it for the sake of my then twelve-year-old, who complained way too often that I didn't get the Chinese poached eggs right. They were either too runny or overdone. But I finally got them perfect after what, maybe fifty attempts?

My other ordinary achievement that I am very pleased with was reverse parking. I have a Mercedes SUV that I love, but the car is impossible to park. Parking lots in European cities are tight. They demand precision and skill. I learned how to drive in Germany while pregnant with my first child. Germany is hands down one of the toughest places in the world to get a driver's license, so I pride myself in being a competent driver. Given that we have the Autobahn, much of which has no speed limit, I have no fear of speed. I can go up to 130 miles per hour without breaking a sweat. However, parallel parking and reverse parking continue to pose a challenge to my eye-hand coordination kung fu. To top it off, parking in my space in the basement of my building is always a hard-fought battle since my space is sandwiched between the wall and my neighbor's ginormous Audi SUV, which never leaves the parking garage.

Four months after moving into the building, I finally nailed the precise angle from which I could slide my car in one clean swoop into my spot, with space on both sides to boot. You may call me too Germanized, nerdy, OCD, or picky—but all those words don't stick. As Andrew Wommack loves to say, it's water off a duck's back,[5] because I know I am tweaking to attain excellence in execution.

Pursuing Excellence versus Perfectionism

My natural DNA of pursuing excellence came to bear during my decade of keeping my nose to the grindstone as a young attorney. This decade was prefaced by surviving a grueling academic curriculum in a cutthroat environment during my four years of law school, where I was at best, mediocre in my grades. By the time I graduated and got a job as a legal apprentice earning almost nothing, I was determined to undo the years of mediocrity and outwork everybody else in the office. It didn't bother me that I was the only young female associate in a boys' club setting. When I hit the race and gender ceiling in my office, I used it to spur me on. I won every single court case thrown at me. My clients couldn't stop praising me in front of my boss, who didn't want to give me a raise. By the time I hit the big league of global law firms, I was trained and conditioned to think deeply and clearly and to consistently deliver work products of excellence. There was no other alternative. In corporate law practice my job was to protect my clients' interests through producing well-drafted documentation, meaning I had to anticipate different scenarios of how things might go sideways. As corporate transactions typically involve immense amounts of money, to the tune of hundreds of millions, there is little room for error. As a matter of fact, it is industry practice to be insured against acts of professional negligence or errors that might cause clients to lose money.

Herein lies the subtle trap: precisely because I was vocationally trained to predict missteps, I was stuck on a treadmill of trying to attain the unattainable—that is, perfection. However, as believers it is key that we discern the difference between reaching for excellence and being bound by perfectionism.

Galatians 3:3 (NLT) brings it right on point:

> **How foolish can you be? After starting your new lives in the Spirit, why are you now trying to become perfect by your own human effort?**

I was straining to attain the unattainable, and I was trapped. Lack of identity, an orphan spirit, the fear of failure, and approval addiction were all drivers of my perfectionism. Thankfully, because of the healing I have received from the Lord and the dramatic renewal of my mind through His Word, today I walk in so much freedom that was inconceivable in my past attorney life.

I now work toward excellence in all that I do, knowing full well that His grace undergirds my endeavors and His wisdom leads my steps. Today, there is a quiet powerful truth inside me signaling, "It's OK to fail; I've got you." Proverbs 24:16 states, "For a righteous man may fall seven times and rise again." It's OK to fail, but kings need to rise again and again and again. There's tremendous security knowing that when you fail, God is there for you, He's your safety net. You can therefore bounce back on your feet and keep trying.

While it's essential not to get stuck on the treadmill trap of perfectionism, it's also essential for kings to reach for excellence. You must ask yourself, "Is my drive powered by faith or fear?" Kings need faith-powered drive. The key to having the right balance is being renewed in your mind through the Word of God. Follow the leading of the Holy Spirit, not the voice of the enemy. Do not let the voice of fear overpower you, but rather focus on God's grace, His overflowing love, His abundant strength, and the covenant promises in His Word.

You need to know His Word. You need the Word to "show you a more excellent way" (1 Cor. 12:31). You need to know the truth of His promises for you. Ephesians speaks of being "filled with all the fullness of God...who is able to do exceedingly abundantly above all that we ask or think, according to the power that works in us" (3:19–20). If that doesn't literally mean infinite power and resources made available to each of us believers, it could well be that we are speaking two different languages this entire time.

As I already pointed out, kings are validated by results. There is no shame in wanting to get results. Excellence in execution gets you results. Tweaking the execution pushes you toward execution excellence. This is the *process to success*. One of my favorite reality series is CNBC's *The Profit*. The host is Marcus Lemonis, who has made it his personal crusade to turn around struggling small businesses and enterprises. He kept his motto crisp and punchy—"people, process, and product." His focus on improving execution in the process results in a vastly improved product for the business. It all comes down to tweaking the execution.

Others who are masters at tweaking include Lisa Su and Jeff Bezos. Lisa Su—one of my personal heroes—is the CEO of semiconductor company Advanced Micro Devices (AMD) and is a genius at tweaking the execution. In one interview on CNBC on July 31, 2019, she mentioned repeatedly, "It's all about the execution...and meeting our commitments."[6] In other TV interviews she often talks about focusing on the right things. She reiterates that it is an ongoing process, and it is a multiyear journey. Her mission and vision are to improve the processes and products at AMD consistently and constantly. AMD was close to bankruptcy when she took over at the helm. Since then, tiny David-like AMD has taken significant market share from the Goliath of semiconductors, Intel. AMD's products have improved phenomenally in quality, and the company has jumped in bottom-line profitability.[7] When I first started trading AMD shares a few years ago, it was at $11 per share, but the stock price was over $90 as of May 2022.[8]

This ability to tweak to get ahead of customer expectations or discontent is what Jeff Bezos aims for every day at Amazon. Bezos' 2017 letter to shareholders was one of the best pieces of motivational writing I have ever read. By founding Amazon, Bezos revolutionized the way we shop and the world we shop in. Since the COVID-19 outbreak, Amazon not only has exploded in terms of revenue but has been critical in deliveries and supplies to millions of homes around the globe. He ended the 2017 shareholder letter by saying, "This year marks the 20th anniversary of our first shareholder letter, and our core values and approach remain unchanged. We continue to aspire to be Earth's most customer-centric company." And the key to Amazon's values and approach? "High standards"—a phrase that appears thirty-five times in the letter. He wrote:

> How do you stay ahead of ever-rising customer expectations? There's no single way to do it—it's a combination of many things. But *high standards* (widely deployed and at all levels of detail) are certainly a big part of it....High standards are contagious.[9]

At Amazon they continue to "obsess" (using Bezos' own word) about customer outcome, which in turn drives the continuous tweaking of their process based on a high-standards culture. It takes great execution to produce a consistent outcome of high standards. How high are your standards in life?

Then there is my friend Kim, who has one of the best business minds I know despite not having finished high school. Her Chinese restaurant Madame Mei is one of the top-rated Chinese fine-dining restaurants in Frankfurt. In addition, she has a hole-in-the-wall Chinese restaurant that caters to volume business. Each of these businesses has a six-figure sales volume each month. Over the years, it has become clear to me that Kim is a genius in gastronomy and business. She can crunch numbers instantly to figure out the cost of each dish on her menu, labor costs, rent, and so on, and she knows how much to sell and how many customers are needed to turn a profit. She has nailed it down to a formula for success. Her key trait is consistency in maintaining excellent standards over decades, day in and day out. She has also trained her team to maintain these standards, irrespective of whether she is physically present to supervise. She is also teachable and open to candid feedback about the food served at her restaurants. She is constantly tweaking the execution and processes in her kitchens to optimize not only sales and inventory but also customer outcomes and satisfaction. She is another master at tweaking the execution and reaching for excellence.

The reach for excellence: Plan, execute, tweak. Repeat. Step and repeat.

Do you see a man who excels in his work? He will stand before kings; he will not stand before unknown men.

—Proverbs 22:29

The Joseph Gold Standard—Faithfulness

The life story of Joseph depicted in the Book of Genesis reveals a man who was the epitome of being faithful, regardless of circumstances. He was a victim of the treachery of his own brothers, sold into slavery, wrongfully thrown into prison, and forgotten by the man who was supposed to repay his kindness. Yet all these things didn't seem to affect his attitude, and he served every one of his masters faithfully. No matter the environment he found himself in, he somehow found the insight and strength to incredulously flip each situation to his advantage—and indeed he even soared above his circumstances and succeeded.

The simplest biblical principles to comprehend are at times the most difficult to apply in life. Being faithful in every season is one of them. Joseph chose not to moan, complain, or even whine throughout. For if he did, it would have been explicitly documented, just as the whining and complaining of the Israelites throughout forty years in the wilderness were meticulously documented—the forty years being a direct consequence of their whining and complaining. Joseph, on the other hand, astoundingly gave his best in every hostile environment in which he was placed. This quality of being consistently faithful, I believe, was a key to unlocking God's favor upon his life, with the result being thousands of lives saved. Note what the Bible says repeatedly about Joseph:

> The LORD was with Joseph, and he was a successful man.
>
> —GENESIS 39:2

> And his master saw that the LORD was with him and that the LORD made all he did to prosper in his hand.
>
> —GENESIS 39:3

> The LORD blessed the Egyptian's house for Joseph's sake; and the blessing of the LORD was on all that he had in the house and in the field.

—GENESIS 39:5

The LORD was with Joseph and showed him mercy.

—GENESIS 39:21

The LORD was with him; and whatever he did, the LORD made it prosper.

—GENESIS 39:23

And Pharaoh said to his servants, "Can we find such a one as [Joseph], a man in whom is the Spirit of God?"

—GENESIS 41:38

The arms of [Joseph's] hands were made strong by the hands of the Mighty God of Jacob…by the God of your father who will help you, and by the Almighty who will bless you with blessings of heaven above.

—GENESIS 49:24–25

Joseph's faithfulness allowed him to win not only his master's favor but also something deeper—his master's trust. Winning his master's trust was key to Joseph's promotion and stepping into authority and oversight in Potiphar's house, in the prison, or all over Egypt.

So Joseph found favor in [Potiphar's] sight, and served him. Then he made him overseer of his house, and all that he had he put under his authority.

—GENESIS 39:4

But the LORD…gave [Joseph] favor in the sight of the keeper of the prison. And the keeper of the prison committed to Joseph's hand all the prisoners who were in the prison; whatever they did there, it was his doing.

—GENESIS 39:21–22

> So [Joseph's] advice was good in the eyes of Pharaoh and in the eyes of all his servants.... Then Pharaoh said to Joseph, "Inasmuch as God has shown you all this, there is no one as discerning and wise as you. You shall be over my house, and all my people shall be ruled according to your word; only in regard to the throne will I be greater than you." And Pharaoh said to Joseph, "See, I have set you over all the land of Egypt."

> Then Pharaoh took his signet ring off his hand and put it on Joseph's hand; and he clothed him in garments of fine linen and put a gold chain around his neck. And he had him ride in the second chariot which he had; and they cried out before him, "Bow the knee!" So he set him over all the land of Egypt. Pharaoh also said to Joseph, "I am Pharaoh, and without your consent no man may lift his hand or foot in all the land of Egypt."

> —GENESIS 41:37, 39–44

The same pattern repeated itself with the warden when Joseph was wrongfully thrown into prison and then again with Pharaoh. When Joseph, after being wrongfully imprisoned and forgotten about for years, was given the opportunity to interpret Pharaoh's dreams, he didn't use the opportunity to complain about his plight. Instead, he knew it was his opportunity to win Pharaoh's favor. Not only did Joseph do his dream interpretation thing perfectly, but he also gave Pharaoh a strategy for the upcoming years of abundance and famine. Pharaoh placed Joseph over all the land of Egypt. The climax of Joseph stewarding his wilderness season faithfully was his promotion to be the prime minister of Egypt. He went from prison to palace in one day.

Here are several key things we can learn from Joseph:

- Consistent faithfulness throughout the toughest seasons of your life unlocks outrageous favor.

- Cut out the drama, and just get it done. Joseph had the ability to stay drama-free, no matter what. I personally know this is not easy but do your best to stay drama-free! Kings do not have time for drama!

- Stop wearing the *victim's crown*. Joseph was clearly the champion victim. Apart from when he was a knucklehead teenager flexing to his brothers prematurely about his calling and destiny, it's fair to say that Joseph landed in one disastrous situation after another through no fault of his own for over two decades. Yet he never lived like a victim nor saw himself as one. Instead, he lived victoriously throughout every difficult season of his life.

- Here's another fundamental truth we believers tend to forget: Life is tough for basically every person on the planet, but those who have a relationship with God has a huge advantage. As a believer, you have access to the infinite power and wisdom of the Holy Spirit—which even Joseph didn't have. So, suck it up and tap into God's gift of strength and wisdom built into your DNA.

- Be loyal to your superiors and employers. Even if your job stinks, stick with it until God shows you clearly otherwise.

- Be faithful to your assignment. At your workplace, focus first and foremost on exceling in your job. Do not try to proselytize or evangelize your coworkers *unsolicited*. This piece of advice is coming from a former evangelist. This is a hard thing for me to say, but I say it only because it is the right thing for you to do. Remember, you were hired to do a job and to do the job well. Your job is the reason you are there. You are not paid to be an evangelist at the workplace. In fact, if you are not performing at your job, any attempts to evangelize will not only make you look bad but all other Christians as well. However, when you succeed at your job and are continually prospering or being promoted, your coworkers and even your boss will want to know the secret of your success, which presents the right moment to give glory to God for your success. I experience that very frequently with people in real estate. Real estate agents are often puzzled as to how I continually manage to get my properties sold above market and crush the bottom-line profit. This is the precise moment I have been waiting for to flex the God muscle. Astoundingly, in recent years, I was given platform after platform in the business world to share the secrets of my success. What glorious opportunities they have been to broadcast God's glory into the world!

- Give it your very best, no matter the circumstance. You honor God when you do so. Focus on getting the results that your employers or superiors are looking for or your coworkers admire, just as Joseph did. Before you know it, you will be primed for promotion. Get ready!

The Other Joseph Gold Standard—Integrity

In the previous section, we examined Joseph's faithfulness. Joseph's other hallmark is integrity, which caused the people he dealt with invariably to like and trust him without question.

Here's the infamous Bible passage in which Potiphar's wife thrust herself shamelessly at Joseph:

And it came to pass after these things that his master's wife cast longing eyes on Joseph, and she said, "Lie with me."

But he refused and said to his master's wife, "Look, my master does not know what is with me in the house, and he has committed all that he has to my hand. There is no one greater in this house than I, nor has he kept back anything from me but you, because you are his wife. How then can I do this great wickedness, and sin against God?"

—GENESIS 39:7–9

Joseph's response to Potiphar's wife reflected the purity of his heart. It brought to my remembrance Proverbs 4:23:

Keep your heart with all diligence, for out of it spring the issues of life.

Even after this honorable attempt from Joseph to reason with her, Potiphar's wife wasn't deterred and came at him every day for some time until the time when Joseph literally had to flee from her. The truth of the matter is Joseph refused to compromise every single time, even when no one was looking. A lesser person would have caved in to the easy seduction at the very first instance, not to mention the multiple other occasions Potiphar's wife threw herself at Joseph. This showed the true caliber and strength of Joseph's character.

Joseph's reward? The Lord continued to be with him and give him favor. Even though Joseph was falsely accused by Potiphar's wife and unjustly thrown into an undoubtedly harsh prison by Potiphar, it didn't stop God's hand from moving on his behalf:

But the LORD was with Joseph and showed him mercy, and He gave him favor in the sight of the keeper of the prison. And the keeper of the prison committed to Joseph's hand all the prisoners who were in the prison; whatever they did there, it was his doing. The keeper of the prison did not look into anything that was under Joseph's authority, because the Lord was with him; and whatever he did, the Lord made it prosper.

—Genesis 39:21–23

Eventually Joseph stepped into his destiny, being appointed by Pharaoh to rule over all of Egypt—all because his integrity caused people to intuitively trust him as well as entrust him with great power and authority. Pharaoh told Joseph:

You shall be over my house, and all my people shall be ruled according to your word; only in regard to the throne will I be greater than you.

—Genesis 41:40

I cannot begin to emphasize how critical it is for us kings to be out in the world representing the kingdom and to always act in integrity. The saying that your reputation will precede you still holds true in every way. Having a reputation of integrity is worth its weight in gold, and it travels far and wide on its own. People want to deal with you, do business with you, and build relationships with you because they know or sense that you are a person of integrity, and they can trust you. Trustworthiness is a rare commodity in this world. Once the element of trust is breached in a relationship, there's no coming back from that.

My late husband was known for being an extremely hard worker; a brilliant lawyer with a quirky, irreverent sense of humor; and someone who always delivered. He was at the top of his game. However, one conversation I had with him impressed me deeply, when he recounted certain remarks made by his high powered client about him. The client said, "That Schmidt, he is one odd guy. He goes to church every Sunday with his family. That's weird. But he's a man of integrity, and you can rely on him 100 percent to be above board in all that he does." I recall radiating with so much pride at that moment. I knew that God was at work deeply in his life in ways that I couldn't see or fathom. Not to downplay his stellar performance as a lawyer, the truth is, it pleased God more than anything that he was a man of integrity.

The other story that he never failed to recount countlessly at dinner parties—naturally with his trademark irreverent humor (and perhaps an element of playful pride)—was about the time a young, beautiful, sexy, adoring law associate threw herself at him, much like Potiphar's wife, while they were working together late at the office. He didn't miss a beat and said the poor quality of her work turned him off all her attempts to flirt with him. In fact, he berated her so sharply for delivering substandard work at 2 a.m. that he reduced her to tears! His trustworthiness was a quality I loved about him. We might have had our issues, but in the department of marital integrity, I knew I could trust him 100 percent.

Here's one final testimony of how integrity in the marketplace paid off for me big time. In my flip business, I sold one of my remodeled apartments in 2019 to a highly satisfied customer who greatly admired my work. She was happy to pay near full asking price, resulting in a handsome profit margin for me. Sometime after closing, the customer contacted me and told me that a potential tenant of hers took it upon herself to measure the square footage of the tiny one-bedroom apartment. She found out that the apartment was marginally smaller than what I had told her when selling the property.

Long story short, I checked in with my attorney and found out that I had the upper hand under German law, despite my unintentional erroneous representation of the size of the property. Fact is, the customer bought the property *as is*. It was on her to conduct a proper appraisal and due diligence of the property, which she failed to do. The market was hot, and she wanted to put in an offer ASAP. Nevertheless, in order not to ruin a good customer relationship and my reputation as a reliable and excellent builder, I offered to return €11,500 to her, even though technically, she didn't have a claim under German law. She accepted my offer readily, and she was so impressed with my sense of integrity that she pursued a friendship with me. She is now working for me part-time as my administrative assistant.

I had won not only a friend but also a trusted, highly competent assistant, a long-awaited answer to my prayers! To top it off, God rewarded my integrity in more ways than one. That €11,500 was made back in my sleep through my stock market investments. And I didn't even break a sweat doing it!

Solomon wrote:

> **A good name [earned by honorable behavior, godly wisdom, moral courage, and personal integrity] is more desirable than great riches; and favor is better than silver and gold.**
>
> —PROVERBS 22:1, AMP

Your reputation is worth more than silver or gold. When you act in integrity repeatedly, favor will chase you down. Once your reputation is sullied or tarnished, it's almost impossible to come back from that.

To sum it up, steward the wilderness season with integrity—it pays!

Adopting the new foundational mindsets and standards will propel you to take territory for God easily. Do not delay! Implement, execute, and watch what God does!

Reform, Govern, and Dominate

*Do the dirty work of reform, clear the debris, and usher in
God's dominion and glory through your leadership.*

The next critical function and assignment of kings is to establish God's dominion on earth. The high calling of kings is to reveal, manifest, and roll out God's kingdom. This goes back to His original mandate and core design for kings set forth in Genesis 1:28:

> **God said to them, "Be fruitful and multiply; fill the earth
> and subdue it; have dominion over...every living thing
> that moves on the earth."**

As I mentioned earlier, when we tie this verse to the metaphor Jesus used in Matthew 13:33, we see that we are God's unstoppable yeast. Kings are God's stealth weapons. Like yeast, kings are wired to continually expand His kingdom until it infiltrates, permeates, and dominates every part of society.

Taking this powerful metaphor one step further, the objective and nature of yeast is not only to permeate the dough entirely but also to transform. While yeast is spreading itself, another process is taking place—transforming the very essence of the dough.

We are mandated and equipped to keep spreading out within the world until we have dominion and transform the nature of society from the inside out.

Kings are called to grow, build, lead, and govern, and although the process can take decades, it will eventually lead to dominion. So, what does it mean to have dominion?

As I mentioned earlier, the Hebrew word for *dominion* in Genesis 1:28 means "to tread down, i.e., subjugate…have dominion, prevail against, reign…rule."[1] Dominion is having the sovereignty, power and authority to lead, shape, govern, regulate, legislate, reform, restructure, control, and influence a demarcated realm, irrespective of whether it is physical, social, or spiritual. God's dominion coming into that demarcated realm will result in the *restoration of God's order in that realm.* The realm will then *flourish*!

Solomon—A Glowing Illustration of Remarkable Leadership and Government

An outstanding illustration of this principle is the reign of King Solomon in the Bible. His reign was clearly a renaissance period in ancient Israel history.

King David unified Israel in an exemplary instance of fulfilling the function and assignment of taking territory for God. His son Solomon, a gifted builder, expanded on his father's legacy in historic proportions. You might say that Solomon corporatized and institutionalized David's kingdom and turned it into one of the most powerful and wealthiest empires of that time. In today's context you might even refer to David as the founder of a start-up venture and Solomon as the CEO who grew the enterprise and took it public. Alternatively, we can compare King David to Steve Jobs, founder of Apple, and Solomon to Tim Cook, the CEO who grew the company into the world's most valuable company, today worth around $2 trillion.[2]

Here are a few observations regarding Solomon's style of ruling that demonstrated he was light years ahead of his time and a remarkable forerunner leader for the ancient world.

First Kings 4 states Solomon had twelve governors in his administration who helped him govern over kingdoms that stretched as far as the Egyptian border. Annexed kingdoms as well as faraway nations in Africa brought tribute to him and served Solomon throughout his reign. For example, the Bible recounts Solomon's visit from a certain queen:

> Now when the queen of Sheba heard of the fame of Solomon concerning the name of the LORD, she came to test him with hard questions. She came to Jerusalem with a very great retinue, with camels that bore spices, very much gold, and precious stones; and when she came to Solomon, she spoke with him about all that was in her heart. So Solomon answered all her questions; there was nothing so difficult for the king that he could not explain it to her. And when the queen of Sheba had seen all the wisdom of Solomon, the house that he had built, the food on his table, the seating of his servants, the service of his waiters and their apparel, his cupbearers, and his entryway by which he went up to the house of the LORD, there was no more spirit in her. Then she said to the king: "It was a true report which I heard in my own land about your words and your wisdom. However I did not believe the words until I came and saw with my own eyes; and indeed the half was not told me. Your wisdom and prosperity exceed the fame of which I heard...." Then she gave the king one hundred and twenty talents of gold, spices in great quantity, and precious stones.

There never again came such abundance of spices as the queen of Sheba gave to King Solomon.

—1 KINGS 10:1–7, 10

There are multiple lessons we can draw from Solomon for today's context, many of which are taught in business schools and practiced by successful corporations around the world today.

- Solomon hired the best people to be around him and provide him with wise counsel and quality advice. Billionaires today such as Ray Dalio are claiming that as a success principle. Personally, I love hiring people who are smarter and more skilled than I am, especially in areas that I am clueless about. I am happy to reward them by paying them generously or above market to express my appreciation in more than mere words.

- Solomon delegated the massive work of running an empire by dividing it up into districts, or subkingdoms, overseen by his top men, the twelve governors. Apart from giving clear parameters for the work to be done and generally maintaining clear communication, I don't micromanage my team or my managers. I leave them to do their work. I also prefer that they show initiative to figure things out and get the job done. The same goes for my home managers and my administrative assistant, whom I am in contact with daily. People love working for and with me, as I give them ample room to do their jobs without constantly looking over their shoulders. This typically results in them being inventive in problem solving and doing a much better job than I could have. It's a win-win situation! However, there must be some balance. Allowing them to be inventive doesn't preclude holding them accountable and expecting them to perform as agreed. "Trust but verify" is a great lesson I picked up from my former business coach JT Foxx.

- Solomon was a master builder. He built teams and systems and could therefore exponentially grow the kingdom David left him, into one capable of creating unprecedented multigenerational wealth through commerce, trading of commodities, precious metals such as gold and silver, royal gifts, tribute money, and taxation. So, what was Solomon's secret sauce?

God gave Solomon wisdom and exceedingly great understanding, and largeness of heart like the sand on the seashore.

—1 KINGS 4:29

In a nutshell, King Solomon dominated! He was best in class when it came to kings. Not only did he grow, build, reform, and govern God's kingdom to unprecedented levels, but he also established God's dominion on earth by catapulting Israel's status in the ancient world to becoming the most powerful nation of that time. The earth was filled with the knowledge of the glory of the Lord because Israel dominated! Solomon ushered in God's order and glory to the earth through his magnificent reign.

For the earth will be filled with the knowledge of the glory of the LORD, as the waters cover the sea.

—HABAKKUK 2:14

Hezekiah—the Brilliant Reformer King Who Changed the Game for Israel

The Bible tells us that King Ahaz, Hezekiah's father, sacrificed to the gods of Damascus since he had been defeated by the Syrians. He believed that by sacrificing to them, these gods would help him. Instead, these gods became "the ruin of him and of all Israel" (2 Chron. 28:23). Not only did Ahaz destroy the articles in the temple, but he also shut up the doors of the temple and "made for himself altars in every corner of Jerusalem. And in every single city of Judah, he made high places to burn incense to other gods, and provoked to anger the LORD God of his fathers" (2 Chron. 28:24–25).

But when Ahaz died, his son Hezekiah took the throne. To me Hezekiah was the most brilliant reformer king in the Old Testament. He took over his father's disastrous reign at the tender age of twenty-five. Yet without delay "he did what was right in the sight of the LORD" (2 Chron. 29:2) and started tackling the enormous mess of an inheritance his father left him. In the very first month of the first year of his reign, "he opened the doors of the house of the LORD and repaired them" (v. 3).

He even functioned as a prophet to the priests and to Israel. He decreed:

> Sanctify yourselves, sanctify the house of the LORD God of your fathers, and carry out the rubbish from the holy place. For our fathers have trespassed and done evil in the eyes of the LORD our God; they have forsaken Him, have turned their faces away from the dwelling place of the LORD, and turned their backs on Him....Therefore the wrath of the LORD fell upon Judah and Jerusalem, and He has given them up to trouble, to desolation, and to jeering.
>
> —2 CHRONICLES 29:5–6, 8

Hezekiah stepped into the position of leadership and directed the priests and the Levites to sanctify themselves and cleanse the house of the Lord by removing the debris and the idols accumulated in the temple over the years.

I can't imagine it was smooth sailing for a young king, newly ascended to the throne, trying to do what was right in the sight of the Lord, particularly after decades of decay and desolation in the nation of Israel. But he did just that, and he did it unflinchingly. To stand up to the old establishment of priests and Levites, Hezekiah had to set his face like flint like the prophet Isaiah (Isa. 50:7), from whom he often sought counsel. Most likely, this old guard was not only his father's loyal subjects but possibly accomplices to his father's corrupt rule. At a minimum they were impotent in persuading King Ahaz to obey God in his leadership of Israel since they were convenient, complicit beneficiaries under Ahaz's rule. And we haven't even gotten started with the rest of Israel and Judah.

Nevertheless, King Hezekiah demonstrated strong, courageous, God-fearing leadership. Then God did the rest:

> **Also the hand of God was on Judah to give them single-ness of heart to obey the command of the king and the leaders, at the word of the LORD.**
>
> —2 CHRONICLES 30:12

The reforms instituted by Hezekiah were as radical as they could get in his time since the life of Israel was centered on religious rituals. Worship was restored in the temple, and sin offerings were made in abundance. Eventually, little by little, "the house of the LORD was set in order" (2 Chron. 29:35). As Hezekiah kept hacking at the mess and reducing it, Israel began to flourish and prosper. Hezekiah sought to obey God wholeheartedly in every work that he did. He was successful in everything he did (2 Chron. 31:21).

There are many lessons that can be learned from King Hezekiah, probably enough to be their own book. Here are some key ones:

Lead with God's vision and direction.

Hezekiah sought God's vision and direction in his leadership and everything that he did. He executed with exceptional clarity and unflinching bullheadedness. That's what it takes. I have personally been called a "bulldog" and a "bulldozer," as compliments on my tenaciousness.

Be powered by God's vision and direction in your leading! The King James Version of Proverbs 29:18 must be engraved within your heart and mind:

> **Where there is no vision, the people perish.**

The Holy Spirit must lead and power you, the king. And once you have God's vision for you as king, do as the prophet Habakkuk said and "write the vision and make it plain on tablets, that he may run who reads it" (Hab. 2:2). In other words, write it down clearly so the people you are leading can take it and run with it.

Clear the debris and lead with integrity.

There should be no compromise ethically or morally in your leadership or business practices. However you label it, accounting engineering or other questionable practices will eventually catch up with you. When you sow seeds of compromise and corruption, you reap the fruits of compromise and corruption.

> **Whatever a man sows, that he will also reap.**
>
> —GALATIANS 6:7

Just the other day I read a Bloomberg article about a billionaire investor/philanthropist who built a private-equity powerhouse but was caught hiding assets and taxable funds in offshore entities and making false declarations on tax returns over a period of fifteen years.[3] God's law and justice will be enforced. Death and taxes are two things that we cannot escape.

As much as I hated doing it, within twenty-four hours of receiving the dreaded estate tax notification, I paid over US$1.5 million in estate taxes for my family in 2020 to the German government. But because I was extremely transparent and collaborative with the tax authorities in the entire process, we were able to wrap up the highly complex and agonizing process in eighteen months, a record time by any standard of tax authorities everywhere.

Integrity matters. "Sow for yourselves righteousness" (Hosea 10:12) and watch what the Lord does.

Strategy can save.

When I visited Israel during the fall of 2018, I learned something about King Hezekiah that was not apparent in the Bible. He was a master strategist and had a brilliant engineering mind. In the time of ancient Israel, water was the most precious commodity, not gold. If you've been to Israel, you will see what I mean. Israel consists of primarily desert terrain with occasional shrubs and green patches that have been developed agriculturally. You feel thirsty all the time in that climate. When an enemy attacked ancient Israel, they only had to cut off the water supply to conduct a successful siege of a city. It would then be defeated and conquered in no time. You will not die without gold, but you most certainly will without water. Water is therefore the most precious commodity there. Protecting a water resource was therefore vital in surviving an attack or winning a battle back in the day.

Second Kings 20:20 mentions in passing that Hezekiah "made a pool and a tunnel and brought water into the city." Similarly, in 2 Chronicles 32:30, right after it says God had given Hezekiah much property, the line was dropped unspectacularly that "Hezekiah also stopped the water outlet of Upper Gihon, and brought the water by tunnel to the west side of the City of David." Anyone reading would have missed this since it sounded exactly like it was part of boring old ancient city planning. Why even mention it at all?

When I arrived at the water tunnel in Israel, which was named after Hezekiah, what I experienced completely blew my mind. The water tunnel was located deep underground, several stories underground in fact. It was pitch-black, narrow, and outright creepy. Together with a Korean lady, I decided to break off from our tour group to explore the tunnel, as I felt the Lord was going to reward me with revelations about King Hezekiah that are fresh from the throne. It took me an hour to get through the creepy tunnel with nothing but the flashlight on my phone wading through the almost icy knee-deep water.

It was constructed deep underground, a remarkably effective way to keep it hidden from view. Hence, they could preserve a key water supply for the city and therefore survive the numerous attacks by the kings of Assyria at that time. Furthermore, I learned that the water was diverted to flow from one point to another using gravity and engineering techniques that were way ahead of its time. I can't get my head around how King Hezekiah was able to devise and implement such a complex civil engineering feat without the drilling and measurement tools we have today. They had to bore through solid stone.

The point is, because of King Hezekiah's intimacy with God and because he constantly sought God's direction and strategy, he was able to save the nation of Israel from enemy attacks through building an ingenious tunnel. What game-changing strategies will the Lord give you when you seek Him?

Put God first; use your authority and ability to form and reform your sphere of influence.

Finally, and most importantly, Hezekiah put God first. He knew firsthand how his father's failure had ruined and devastated the nation, and it was incumbent upon him, the new ruler God had placed on the throne, to make things right. Because he did, he flourished and prospered with no end in sight, and so did Israel.

When you are a king, you have the inherent authority and ability to make things right with God in your realm, or sphere of influence. Only you, as the chosen king and leader, can elevate Him to His rightful status, be it in your family, your home, your business, the department where you work, or the town where you've been elected to office. You have the authority and ability to place God over and above everything else.

That was the choice of Truett Cathy, the founder of Chick-fil-A. Recall that I mentioned Chick-fil-A's corporate purpose, engraved on a plaque outside its headquarters:

> **To glorify God by being a faithful steward of all that is entrusted to us. To have a positive influence on all who come in contact with Chick-fil-A.[4]**

That was also the choice of the Tang family in Singapore, known for owning vast businesses and prime real estate in the island nation I used to call home. At the bottom of their flagship thirty-three-story building, Tang Plaza, there is a small, inconspicuous plaque on the ground floor. I had never noticed it before, but on my last visit, in August 2018, in the middle of a busy errand day, the Holy Spirit stopped me in my tracks, directing me to take a pause and take a picture of the plaque. It read:

Tang Plaza

Named in honour of Mr Tang Choon Keng and the late Mrs Tang Sok Kiar

Dedicated to the Lord Jesus Christ 17 February 1995

To God Be the Glory

From Truett Cathy to the Tangs to Lisa Su transforming AMD to my husband helping to elevate his law firm to the top of the ranks in Europe, kings can change their spheres of influence. It takes sacrifice, and it is hard. But as a reformer king, your call is to step up and transform your ruling sphere into the best version that God has placed in your heart. You will never be happy until you have accomplished that.

CHAPTER 7

Help Build the Temple and Advance the Kingdom

Kings hold the keys.

B e warned. This chapter is a total minefield of hard truths. If need be, put down the book and go for a walk. Or you can just throw caution to the wind and jump right in.

Kings must help build the temple—the body of Christ—and advance the kingdom. There is no getting around it. Because we are hardwired to be problem solvers and critical thinkers, we can spot a hundred flaws about our local church or the body of Christ at large and come up with infinite reasons that they do not deserve our support and especially our money if we go by metrics in the non-church world. I know because I have walked down this path before. My late husband and I have been around the same block many times—a never-ending back-and-forth about the missteps of churches and ministries in financial management. Why then should we give money to them at all when they are clueless financially?

Herein lies the answer—there is no getting around what is in the Bible about the role of kings vis-à-vis the temple.

King Solomon's mandate and assignment from God was to build the temple. That's exactly what Solomon did. In fact, he accumulated so much wealth that he didn't break a sweat building the temple, a temple that had to be meticulously built with astronomical amounts of gold and silver.

Solomon's mandate was clear:

> The LORD spoke to my father David, saying, "Your son, whom I will set on your throne in your place, he shall build the house for My name."
>
> —1 KINGS 5:5

> Then the word of the LORD came to Solomon, saying: "Concerning this temple which you are building, if you walk in My statutes, execute My judgments, keep all My commandments, and walk in them, then I will perform My word with you, which I spoke to your father David. And I will dwell among the children of Israel, and will not forsake My people Israel."
>
> —1 KINGS 6:11–13

Solomon fulfilled his assignment by building the temple perfectly and by obediently following God's directions to the letter. Apparently, it took him seven years to build and complete the temple (1 Kings 6:38), of which just the gold and silver would have been worth over $226 trillion today.[1]

It didn't stop there either. He made astronomical offerings and sacrifices to the temple, so much so that they were referred to using the term *multitude*:

> Also King Solomon, and all the congregation of Israel who were assembled with him, were with him before the

ark, sacrificing sheep and oxen that could not be counted or numbered for multitude.

—1 KINGS 8:5

And then there was the result of all his investment:

And it came to pass, when the priests came out of the holy place, that the cloud filled the house of the LORD, so that the priests could not continue ministering because of the cloud; for the glory of the LORD filled the house of the LORD.

—1 KINGS 8:10–11

And just as with King Solomon, the mandate of kings today is ultimately about building the temple, the body of Christ, through the accumulation of astronomical wealth to prepare the bride of Christ for the coming of her Bridegroom. Kings hold the keys to building the temple.

And in the era of global pandemic, Russian invasions, sharp political divide, and impending global recession, am I imagining things, or has the end-time clock been dramatically hastened? National governments all over the world in 2020 to 2021 seemed to agree too easily with one another on shutting down entire economies and closing borders, with hardly any government challenging the insanity of it all or the overreaction of almost every government on the planet. Why didn't any world leader question the constitutionality of draconian measures that severely restricted one's freedom of movement in lockdowns? No government has been held accountable whatsoever for these measures nor the decimation of entire economies! Why were the political leaders of countless nations so willing to defer and submit to unelected public health officials and cower in the face of science? When did science become the arbitrary sledgehammer answer for anyone that disagrees with shutdowns of economies? Doesn't today's scenario hint at the beginnings of the one-world system?

Elon Musk has a startup called Neuralink, which in August 2020 unveiled plans for a brain-implant device allowing users to control computers with their minds.[2] But when implanted in humans, what is there to stop the artificial intelligence (AI) computers from reversing function and controlling the human brain or manipulating human will and consciousness instead? Where does that leave free will or the human soul?

In fact, many AI scientists are pushing toward *singularity*, when AI abilities overtake the abilities of the human brain, potentially allowing AI to have control of all aspects of life as we know it, because they deem artificial intelligence as ultimately superior and more efficient than human intelligence. You might think it's just the few oddball scientists and thinkers pushing for this, but not when they are the likes of Elon Musk or Jeff Bezos, both of whom being the top two wealthiest men in the world, have billions to move and shape the planet and civilization as they see fit. Last I heard, both are looking to colonize space or other planets for human habitation as a solution to problems on earth.[3]

How do we as kingdom people counter all these seemingly insane, unbiblical, yet insurmountable growing trends?

We need a generation of young kings who are brilliant in coding and business and are sold-out for Jesus to access Silicon Valley incubator money so that technology can be developed to counter Neuralink-type initiatives, to slow down the end-time clock. We need the likes of the coding team behind the ubiquitous YouVersion Bible app, which has been downloaded almost 450 million times around the world in 1,372 languages.[4] I have no doubt that the brilliant developer of The Bible App, Bobby Gruenewald, will have a big mansion in heaven when we all gather one day in eternity.

I try to do my part in investing companies with critical technology as led by the Holy Spirit. In early 2021, I felt compelled to invest a quarter million seed capital into a tech startup in Minnesota called Boon Logic, Inc. that recently concluded a $6 million raise successfully. This company provides best-in-class algorithmic breakthrough technology solutions in unsupervised machine learning critical in big industry from pharmaceutical and cloud computing to mining and oil and gas. After I decided to commit funds, I was stunned to find out that many of their C-suite execs, including the cofounder, CEO, and CTO, are all strong believers sold out for Jesus! That cannot be a coincidence; it's more like a Holy Ghost setup!

There is an acute urgency for kings to arise, to fight, to flourish, and to recover and take back from the enemy their God-given corners of the world, whether in tech, business, politics, or academia, the final being a sphere of influence that has sadly been ceded to the enemy with barely a fight.

When God's kings wield influence and enjoy unlimited resources at our fingertips, we can move and deploy funds and resources to protect the kingdom and His people as the times become increasingly dark.

As I write this segment in late 2020, an unprecedented war is still being waged over the 2020 US presidential election. Obscene amounts of money were spent by both Democrats and Republicans in the campaign running up to the election. So much power has been ceded to the media that they can blindside millions, even billions.

Imagine just for a moment having access to resources of such scale and proportion. What kind of possibilities would open up for God's plans to make headway and be established on earth? We would then have the outright ability and power to change the narrative, move the needle, tip the scales.

The Elephant in the Room

But for kings to effectively build the temple and advance the kingdom, there is the elephant in the room that needs to be addressed.

Kings and priests do not get along.

There is a huge, awkward, unspoken divide. But it had to be said.

I recall how Mario used to complain for years that the pastors in the churches we attended either ignored him or neglected to build a relationship with him. For the record, we weren't church hoppers … we attended one for eleven years. It took a lot of persuasion on my part to get him to church in the first place, but when he finally showed up, the pastor barely noticed he was there, even though I was one of the ministry leaders then. Pastors came and went, each staying for about three or four years, but none gave him the time of day.

Kings also need to be pastored and shepherded. Most pastors or priests do not know how to shepherd a king. In a recent conversation, an insightful fellow minister revealed to me that many pastors feel insecure about approaching the wealthier and more successful non-clergy members of their congregations. Many ministers feel inferior to them, so they avoid them at all costs. Some, to feel better about their poverty and lack and their inability to change that, go all religious and pharisaical on the successful, wealthy members of their parish, making them feel less than or unwelcome. Ever wonder why kings are few and far between at Sunday services in most churches? Why would kings ever want to attend church when they are so unwelcome?

In a recent conversation, someone pointed out the other extreme she's witnessed in her church. The wealthy members in her church have too much sway and influence over her church leadership, amounting to unfair favoritism behavior that was reprimanded by James in James 2:1–7. There is an imbalance in the body, and it must be addressed. Wealthy church members shouldn't be focusing their influence in churches (unless appointed to specific ministry positions), but as kings they ought to divert their influence outside church doors instead and spearhead God's impact deep into the world.

Whatever it is—divide, disunity, imbalance—it must stop. Course correction must take place.

Solomon was in harmonious collaboration with his priests. Together they were dedicated to *united* worship of the one true God. The king and the priests were perfectly *united*.

Truth be told, kings and priests hold *equal* weighting in the Bible. Take a fresh look with me at Zechariah 4. It pays to pore over verses 8–14:

> Moreover the word of the LORD came to me, saying: "The hands of Zerubbabel have laid the foundation of this temple; his hands shall also finish it. Then you will know that the LORD of hosts has sent Me to you. For who has despised the day of small things? For these seven rejoice to see the plumb line in the hand of Zerubbabel. They are the eyes of the LORD, which scan to and fro throughout the whole earth."
>
> Then I answered and said to him, "What are these two olive trees—at the right hand of the lampstand and at its left?" And I further answered and said to him, "What are these two olive branches that drip into the receptacles of the two gold pipes from which the golden oil drains?"
>
> ...So he [the angel] said, "these are the two anointed ones who stand beside the Lord of the whole earth."

In the Amplified translation, it was interpreted as "These are the two sons of fresh oil [Joshua the high priest and Zerubbabel the prince of Judah] who are standing by the Lord of the whole earth [as His anointed ones]."

Zerubbabel was appointed as governor to lead the Israelites exiled in Babylon to return to Jerusalem. He was tasked with the rebuilding of the temple, and he functioned as the king or political leader of the returning Jews. Zerubbabel's bloodline is a kingly one. He was the grandson of Jehoiachin, the last king of Judah before the Babylonian conquest and subsequent destruction of the temple in 587/586 BC that resulted in the exile of the Israelites in Babylon for seventy years.

Two keys are embedded in this passage. The first key is the olive trees are representative of the two leadership offices, that of the priest and that of the king. The high priest Joshua held the priestly office over Israel while Zerubbabel as governor held the political or kingly rulership of Israel at that time. When the angel of the Lord in verse 14 said, "These are the two anointed ones, who stand beside the Lord of the whole earth," the angel was actually saying they were the two most important helpers of Jesus Christ and were ruling alongside Christ in equivalent power and authority. There is no mention whatsoever that one office is more important or less important than the other. They stand beside the Lord. They have equal weighting vis-à-vis each other's office. This was repeated in Revelation 11:4 by Jesus Himself:

> These [witnesses] are the two olive trees and the two lampstands which stand before the God of the earth.

Again, the *equal* standing of the two witnesses before the Lord, the kingly office and the priestly office, is implicit here.

The second key is there is a prophetic message embedded in chapter 4 that is relevant today. Just like Zerubbabel, kings are tasked with the rebuilding of the temple: "The hands of Zerubbabel have laid the foundation of this temple; his hands shall also finish it" (v. 9).

Kings are *key* to the rebuilding of the body of Christ. They are key to foundation building; they are key to finishing and getting the job done. They can no longer stay in exile, away from the temple, because the seventy years of captivity have expired. The message for kings to return to the temple ties in with my third vision, where innumerable kings are ascending a flight of massive steps and heading towards the temple.

Kings are key, but when kings collaborate with priests, a powerful, heaven-ordained symbiosis is consummated.

Hezekiah is chronicled in Israel's history to be one of the most effective, righteous, and successful kings to rule Judah. I call him the best reformer king in Israel's history. I pointed out earlier that Hezekiah often sought the counsel of the prophet Isaiah, who was his contemporary, as laid out in 2 Kings 19. I believe they had a powerful behind-the-scenes king-prophet collaboration that may not be apparent when we are reading the Bible. I believe he wouldn't have been this successful or effective in his reign and reforms of Judah without the strategies or counsel from God sent through the prophet Isaiah. This mirrors the collaboration that is essential between apostles and prophets, who together are also unstoppable in building the foundation of the church. Similarly, when kings and priests unite, they are unstoppable, not to mention that kings are totally, 100 percent apostolic in function.

As I said, course correction must take place. The divide must dissolve. The healing and unification between kings and priests must begin. There is no time to lose.

The Father wants to call out His kings to establish His plans not just by sending out evangelistic missions but by establishing kingdom *dominion on earth*. Before He ascended into heaven, Jesus spoke these words, known as the Great Commission:

> **All authority has been given to Me in heaven and on earth. Go therefore and make disciples of all the nations, baptizing them in the name of the Father and of the Son and of the Holy Spirit, teaching them to observe all things that I have commanded you; and lo, I am with you always, even to the end of the age.**

—MATTHEW 28:18–20

Lance Wallnau brought clarity to this passage in a way I had not considered before. Jesus said we are to make disciples of entire *nations*, not people, meaning we can have dominion of entire systems.[5] Therefore, we are to make disciples *of* the nations, not *within* the nations.

Under the umbrella of the Holy Spirit, kingdom dominion on earth can be established only through wealth and influence amassed and wielded by God's kings rising. This is a monumental task, and the kings need the support of priests to accomplish the assignment. When the church arises in these areas, kings and priests united will *spearhead* the advance of the kingdom, and the glory of God will overflow from the body of Christ, filling the earth with His glory, "as the waters cover the sea" (Hab. 2:14). That's when the long-awaited massive revival will break out among the nations.

One final observation before we meet again in Part II. This message is not just another inner healing, turning curses to blessings book. This is, at its core, a groundswell, grassroots movement of kings rising from the ashes, coming out of Babylonian exile to fulfill the lifetime assignment of rebuilding the temple and advancing the kingdom.

Kings hold the keys.

PART II
WEALTH

A s you begin to step into your kingly calling and anointing, as you plow, grind, and battle, you will begin to accumulate wins and flourish in your appointed sphere. Wealth will intrinsically and naturally flow through your hands. I hope it is clear by now the message of Kings and Wealth has never been about wealth building per se but about uncovering your true identity and restoring it to your forebrain, your conscious thought life, to the intentionality that your high calling deserves.

In the last two years, the world has been sucked into fear and uncertainty at every turn. Now, even as the pandemic is fading at the time of writing, we are faced with new crises—the rise of Russian and Chinese imperialism (the war in Ukraine is still raging), rising oil prices, historically high inflation, extreme market volatility, and possible global recession—the list goes on. It wouldn't be an overstatement to describe the past two years as the darkest it has been in a long time, and it will continue to be so for some time to come.

But the irony is, the darker it gets, the more even a tiny beam of light can pierce through and disrupt the darkness. You are that tiny disrupting beam.

> **Darkness shall cover the earth...but the LORD will arise over you, and His glory will be seen upon you. The Gentiles shall come to your light, and kings to the brightness of your rising.... You shall see and become radiant, and your heart shall swell with joy; because the abundance of the sea shall be turned to you, the wealth of the Gentiles shall come to you.... They shall bring gold and incense, and they shall proclaim the praises of the LORD.**

> —ISAIAH 60:2–3, 5–6

This is the time for believers to arise, shine and let that light pierce through and disrupt this dark age, and to attract the long-time-coming, elusive transfer of wealth from the wicked into the hands of the godly. Remember, kings hold the keys to usher in kingdom dominion on earth, and wealth is the weapon to do just that.

Five Keys for the Wealth Anointing

In the years of building wealth together with my late husband, I identified five powerful keys to tap into the wealth anointing that is an integral part of our inheritance as Christ followers:

> 1. Know your source, your covenant, and your spiritual ancestry.
> 2. Know your purpose.
> 3. Work your hands.
> 4. Steward your finances faithfully and shrewdly.
> 5. Sow with strategy; expect return.

Kings on the rise, take note!

CHAPTER 8

Know Your Source, Your Covenant, and Your Ancestry

Don't fear. There's always more.

The first key to tapping into the wealth anointing is to know your source, your covenant, and your ancestry. Knowing and understanding these three components lays the groundwork for the other spiritual keys.

Know Your Source

Getting to know your source, who is God Himself, and the covenant He swore over you is the quintessential key.

Knowing the heart of your Father will ground you and transform you. Did you know that your heavenly Father watches over you intimately and closely in every way, much like a young dad watches over his toddler? Psalm 121 beautifully depicts not only the protectiveness of the Father over His sons and daughters but also that He is literally the Creator of the discernible and indiscernible universe. Getting a glimpse of His infinity releases deep security within our cores. Nothing can displace us from the love and protection of our Father, who has the universe in the palm of His Hand.

> I will lift up my eyes to the hills—from whence comes my help? My help comes from the LORD, who made heaven and earth. He will not allow your foot to be moved; He who keeps you will not slumber. Behold, He who keeps Israel shall neither slumber nor sleep. The LORD is your keeper; the LORD is your shade at your right hand. The sun shall not strike you by day, nor by the moon by night. The LORD shall preserve your soul. The LORD shall preserve your going out and your coming in from this forth, and even forevermore.
>
> —PSALM 121

This passage anchors me in my very core.

Another classic passage we tend to gloss over due to over familiarity is the parable of the prodigal son. Too often we focus on the sons in the parable, be it the returning prodigal son or the insecure, performance-driven older son. But it is the father character that I am drawn towards.

> And he arose and came to his father. But when he was still a great way off, his father saw him and had compassion, and ran and fell on his neck and kissed him. And the son said to him, "Father, I have sinned against heaven and in your sight, and am no longer worthy to be called your son." But the father said to his servants, "Bring out the best robe and put it on him, and put a ring on his hand and sandals on his feet....Let us eat and be merry; for this my son was dead and is alive again;..."
>
> —LUKE 15:20–24

The image of the father in the parable rejoicing and running without restraint toward his once-rebellious but now-repentant son, with no mention of past sins and wrongdoing but instead having compassion and embracing him is beyond moving. Until this day, this image continues to cut me to the core. On his own accord, the father went even further and restored his estranged son to his position as an heir, which his son clearly no longer deserved but in fact intentionally abandoned. This is grace in action. This is the heart of the Father revealed.

My own earthly father was broken in every way imaginable. Years of witnessing abuse within the family left me with stubborn scars. Only when I was rooted in the infinitely secure love of our heavenly Father could I reach out in 2010 to my earthly father, whom I had barely seen in two decades, in genuine forgiveness and grace. Within two years of our reconciliation, my father received Christ into his heart after a lifetime of pagan worship of Buddha, idols, and even a dead fetus. He was saved at the age of seventy-nine and baptized at eighty-two.

Like the prodigal son, kings must know they too have been restored as heirs and their heavenly Father can't wait for them to step into all they are ordained to inherit.

These are Jesus' own words:

> What man is there among you who, if his son asks for bread, will give him a stone? Or if he asks for a fish, will he give him a serpent? If you then, being evil, know how to give good gifts to your children, how much more will your Father who is in heaven give good things to those who ask Him!
>
> —MATTHEW 7:9–11

These two passages in Luke and Matthew undeniably portray the giving nature of the Father. Our Father is a giver, regardless of whether we deserve what He has for us, because we do not and will never deserve it. Yet that is the quintessential definition of grace—it is undeserved and unmerited. God is a giver of good gifts (Jas. 1:17), and He does not withhold any good thing.

> For the LORD God is a sun and a shield; the LORD will give grace and glory; no good thing will He withhold from those who walk uprightly.
>
> —PSALM 84:11

The truth is He didn't even withhold His Son from us.

> If God is for us, who can be against us? He who did not spare His own Son, but delivered Him up for us all, how shall He not with Him also freely give us all things?
>
> —ROMANS 8:31–32

Hence there is always more where that came from...infinitely more—more love, more grace, more abundance, more of all things good. Not to mention, we are also heirs with access to His infinite storehouse and economy. Once we grasp this truth, we step into the abundance mindset, which is a great segue into the next segment, knowing your covenant.

Know Your Covenant

The Abrahamic covenant has no strings attached, no limit, and no bottom, and it's yours if you believe. The legal definition of a covenant can fill up a page, but in its essence it's a promise. A covenant can take the form of either a conditional or *unconditional* promise and is found in every agreement that is enforceable by law.

The covenant that God made with Abraham, to which we are bound through the spiritual bloodline of Jesus Christ, is an *unconditional unilateral* covenant:

> I will make you a great nation; I will bless you and make your name great; and you shall be a blessing. I will bless those who bless you, and I will curse him who curses you; and in you all the families of the earth shall be blessed.

—Genesis 12:2–3

I will make you exceedingly fruitful; and I will make nations of you, and kings shall come from you. And I will establish My covenant between Me and you and your descendants...for an everlasting covenant....Also I give to you and your descendants after you the land in which you are a stranger, all the land of Canaan, as an everlasting possession; and I will be their God.

—Genesis 17:6–8

These two lynchpin passages are the premise of a few takeaways. First, God made this covenant with us *unconditionally and unilaterally*. Unconditionality is contrary to human nature. Most of what people give or offer has strings or a price attached. The idea that there's no such thing as a free lunch is what most of us are accustomed to thinking our whole lives. The truth is it's the total opposite of God's covenant with you, borne out of His covenant with Abraham. In Genesis 12, God called Abraham not only literally but unilaterally. Out of the blue, God said to Abram (Abraham's name before God changed it), "Get out of your country, from your family and from your father's house, to a land that I will show you" (v. 1).

To help you understand the nature of God's covenant better, let's look at the legal context. A covenant in an agreement typically requires the fulfillment by both parties to that covenant. That is not the case with the covenant given to Abram by God—its fulfillment was solely dependent on God, unilaterally and unconditionally. Abram was seventy-five years old at that time. He didn't ask to be made into a great nation. He was *simply chosen*, and God made him the father of nations, hence the name Abraham. In fact, in Genesis 15, God performed a ceremony to seal the covenant with Abram by passing between two halves of animals. While all this happened, Abram was in a deep sleep (Gen. 15:12, 17).[1] When I first studied this chapter in 2009, the entire chapter seemed like gibberish to me, but now it is clear that God demonstrated the unilateral and solitary nature of His covenant by sealing the covenant while Abram slept. Where am I going with this? YOU do not need to earn this covenant; it's dropped into your lap just like it was with Abram!

This brings us to the next point—since this is a promise made by God, a passage in Numbers comes to mind immediately:

> **God is not a man that He should lie....Has He said, and will He not do? Or has He spoken, and will He not make it good?...He has blessed, and I cannot reverse it.**
>
> —NUMBERS 23:19–20

A promise by God is always and without fail irreversible. In fact, the Bible radically states,

> **And GOD said, "...I'll *make* every word I give you come true."**
>
> —JEREMIAH 1:12, MSG, EMPHASIS ADDED

God Himself will guarantee the performance of His Word! You can't get a better backer than that!

Then, 430 years later, God gave Moses a conditional covenant, or the Law, to help him govern the unruly, newly freed Israelite slaves who escaped Egypt. However, this latter covenant given to Moses does not in any way supersede or erase the unconditional, unilateral Abrahamic covenant. The Mosaic covenant, or the Law, could only be fulfilled by Jesus' work on the cross. In fact, Paul hit the nail on the head when he wrote:

> **This is what I am trying to say: The agreement God made with Abraham could not be canceled 430 years later when God gave the law to Moses. God would be breaking his promise.**
>
> —GALATIANS 3:17, NLT

Don't get me wrong: I don't know it all, but it is dawning more and more on me how little I have truly experienced of His covenant blessings. The deeper and further I push, the more I realize that there is no bottom and there is no limit.

How do you benefit from this amazing covenant? As a born-again believer in Jesus Christ, you are plugged into the Abrahamic covenant. You know the phrase *plug and play*? It is an apt description of what you have. It's Christianity 101: you are a joint heir with Christ, and you have been grafted into the Abrahamic covenant like a wild olive tree because of your union with Jesus:

> **The Spirit Himself bears witness with our spirit that we are children of God, and if children, then heirs—heirs of God and joint heirs with Christ.**
>
> —ROMANS 8:16–17

> **And you Gentiles, who were branches from a wild olive tree, have been grafted in. So now you all receive the blessing God has promised Abraham and His children, sharing in the rich nourishment from the root of God's special olive tree.**
>
> —ROMANS 11:17, NLT

Let's circle back to Genesis now that we have established that you are equally entitled to what Abraham received from God and that we get to have what Jesus has (which is unfathomable as far as our puny intellect is concerned). What then has God promised Abraham and therefore you? What are the parameters of the promise?

God said He will make *your* name great. This keeps getting amplified within that passage alone, as all people on earth will be blessed through you (Gen. 12:3). It gets better.

Later, in Genesis 17:4–8, God changed Abram's name to Abraham, meaning father of nations, and specifically promised to make

Abram, and therefore *you*, "exceedingly fruitful," to bring kings from his and *your* bloodline, to establish an eternal covenant with him and *you*, and my favorite, He promised to give Abraham and therefore *you*, His heir, land as an everlasting possession.

Did you know God gave *you* the right to own real estate from as far back as the time of Abraham? I am taking a leap here, but however you look, these promises seem outrageous. Based on a simplistic, linear, no-need-to-read-between-the-lines reading of Genesis, there is no limit to what God wants to bless you with. As my fourteen-year-old used to say, "In your face!" You are going to be in-your-face exceedingly fruitful. Bam! You are going to have land as an everlasting possession. No disclaimers, no qualifiers, simply in-your-face outrageous promises.

Know Your Spiritual Ancestry

Your spiritual ancestors are biblical billionaires, unlike your broke biological ancestors. You come from a spiritual lineage of billionaires. Let's take a look.

Abraham the patriarch

The first billionaire in your lineage is obviously Abraham. Abraham had tons of gold and silver. He was clearly a successful rancher since he had immense livestock, so much so that he and his nephew Lot couldn't dwell in the same land (Gen. 13:2–6). Did I mention he's just like Liam Neeson in *Taken* but better? That's because he had a private army of 318 soldiers to do the work for him! They were effective like modern-day marines and managed to rescue his nephew Lot and his family who were captured by sinister warlords (Gen. 14). And how can I forget? Abraham was a big-time real estate owner. All of Canaan (more land than today's Israel) was his; he landed the mother of all land grants by God Almighty Himself. By today's standards, I guesstimate he would be at the very least a decabillionaire—a person with tens of billions as his net worth.

Solomon, the 2-trillion-dollar man

Solomon had immense wisdom. He asked God for wisdom instead of wealth, but God rewarded him with ridiculous wealth anyways because of his integrity.

Solomon was so wealthy and had so much gold that silver was not worth anything in his time.

> The king made silver as common in Jerusalem as stones.
>
> —1 KINGS 10:27

He had 666 talents of gold (1 Kings 10:14), or 22 tons of gold, coming to him in a year. That amount of gold is worth over 1 billion dollars today. Guess what? He ruled for forty years, so you can do the math.

Apparently, at his peak, his fortune would be valued at $2 trillion today.[2] King Solomon is our 2-trillion-dollar man, ranked the fifth richest person in human history. Not too shabby for a spiritual ancestor.

Jesus, the man Himself

Abraham and Solomon are just the tip of the iceberg when it comes to being our indisputable wealthy biblical ancestors. That leads us to the burning question: What about Jesus Himself?

Jesus is often portrayed as broke. Certain verses are popularly quoted or taken out of context, to portray that Jesus walked the earth as a hobo. For example:

> Foxes have holes and birds of the air have nests, but the Son of Man has nowhere to lay His head.
>
> —LUKE 9:58

This is my view. In that context Jesus was replying to a scribe who said he would follow Jesus. Jesus' reply to the scribe was strong and borders on exaggeration and hyperbole to drive home the point, to count the cost of what it means to be a disciple of Jesus. Jesus was using that phrase to communicate to him that he too, like Jesus, would have to give up ordinary earthly comforts to do God's work. As God's mission will always take priority, his life would no longer be comfortable, but it didn't necessarily mean we would be broke.[3]

Another commonly abused verse is in Philippians:

> **When the time came, he set aside the privileges of deity and took on the status of a slave, became human!**
>
> —PHILIPPIANS 2:7, MSG

However, if the passage where this verse was found is read in its entirety, then it would read very differently. The Amplified version brings much needed clarity and is worth repeating.

> **Have this same attitude in yourselves which was in Christ Jesus [look to Him as your example in selfless humility], who, although He existed in the form and unchanging essence of God [as One with Him, possessing the fullness of all the divine attributes—the entire nature of deity], did not regard equality with God a thing to be grasped or asserted [as if He did not already possess it, or was afraid of losing it]; but emptied Himself [without renouncing or diminishing His deity, but only temporarily giving up the outward expression of divine equality and His rightful dignity] by assuming the form of a bond-servant, and being made in the likeness of men [He became completely human but was without sin, being fully God and fully man].**
>
> —PHILIPPIANS 2:5–7, AMP

Paul's focal point here was to tackle the attitude of the believers, exhorting them to be humble like Jesus; even though all heaven and earth belonged to Jesus, He didn't hesitate to lay that aside (including His expression of deity) to be able to walk among men as fully human. Paul was comparing Jesus' time as a human being to His preincarnate form. The step down for Jesus was so inconceivably enormous that he used the analogy of a slave in Roman times, a human with no legal personhood who was open to corporal punishment and exploitation of every depraved kind. In other words, the magnitude of what Jesus gave up in taking on human form is something that we as humans can never understand. Leaving so much behind in heaven to embrace what He had on earth is somewhat comparable to a person becoming a slave in that time. Even that doesn't fully capture the loss He endured.

And to better grasp what He lost, we need to understand who the Son of Man is and what He had. The Amplified version of Philippians 2 emphasized the fullness of deity of Jesus extremely well, and Hebrews 1:2 also drives home the same point:

> **...His Son, whom He has appointed heir of all things, through whom also He made the worlds.**

> —HEBREWS 1:2

If everything belongs to Jesus, what has He got to prove? Does it matter that He looked like a hobo when He had the universe at His fingertips? He might have looked like one, but He wasn't one. Let's check out the evidence.

In Matthew 17:27, Jesus paid taxes for Himself and His crew by pulling money out of a fish. Why would He need to carry cash when a fish could become an ATM at His command?

In John 6:4–14, Jesus fed five thousand people with five loaves and two fish. At the end of the miraculous meal, they had twelve baskets of bread left over. Have you wondered why that is the case? It's a lot of leftovers! That can't be overlooked. It's not like Jesus was incapable of executing a miracle precisely. He could have calculated it to the precise crumb if He wanted to! But instead, He chose to do a miracle with twelve baskets of leftovers. Isn't that a lot of excess? My traditionally Chinese mom would have remarked, "What a waste!"

Here is what I think was happening. In this miracle, He gave a live demonstration of the proportions and scale that He was accustomed to—that is, *infinity*. In fact, I would describe Jesus as a *minimalist* who operated in *exponential* multiples. In that incident, He was demonstrating an ordinary day in the life of the Son of God—overflow overdrive. Let's do the math. A conservative estimate is that Jesus was probably feeding ten thousand men, women, and children (women and children were not recorded at the time, but they were present and had to be fed). This would have required approximately twenty thousand fish, assuming that each person ate two fish. Don't forget they only had two fish to work with. Those two fish multiplied ten thousand times to feed everyone present. This is an increase of 1,000,000 percent. This is the kind of multiple that Jesus operated in. We haven't even gotten started on the bread that ended with twelve baskets of leftovers—that's an infinite multiple by any stretch! The point is the Son of Man operates only in exponential multiples. Why are we so fearful when He moves in such scale and proportion? He didn't say be frugal and simplify; He said be fruitful and multiply!

To recap, Jesus had instantaneous access into the dimension of resources. Earthly treasures are nothing to Him since He is the heir and owner of *all*. Since that's the case, it didn't matter that He looked like a hobo. People who have it don't need to flaunt it. Warren Buffet lives in a modest house that is worth only .001 percent of his total wealth.[4] The religious camp got it wrong.

Even as I write, I am kicking myself about how limiting I am in my own thought life! I forget, like everyone else, that we come from ancestry that operates in limitless scale and exponential multiples.

CHAPTER 9

Know Your Purpose

When you're not in service to God, you can end up being in service to everything else.

—Kanye West

According to Investopedia, "Wealth is an accumulation of valuable economic resources that can be measured in terms of either real goods or money value. Net worth is the most common measure of wealth, determined by taking the total market value of all physical and intangible assets owned, then subtracting all debts."[1]

This economics definition of wealth is highly accurate and highly boring. It conjures up an image of a mechanical, emotionless, repetitive process of accumulation of resources. On the same website, it specifically identifies a person of wealth as a high-net-worth individual, somebody with at least $1 million dollars in liquid assets, like cash or cash equivalent.[2] In other words, if a person's wealth is only expressed numerically on bank balances and statements, then the person's identity is reduced to essentially numbers and zeros behind a person's name. But God has a better plan for wealth itself.

Imagine having a million dollars at your disposal. Wouldn't the idea alone bring you to a place of financial peace and freedom? But imagine possessing that first million and more. What can you do for your family? What can you do for God, His kingdom and His people? Suddenly wealth takes on a new expression, not just in numbers and zeros but in the form of heavenly missions manifesting on earth.

When we begin to comprehend and apprehend His purpose and vision for us to build wealth, we will accumulate resources not to serve ourselves, which gets boring and meaningless in no time, but to serve God and the execution of His plans on earth.

The fact is, sending the gospel to the ends of the world, or even your local area, requires funding. Every mission needs money—from discipleship programs to feeding the poor, housing refugees, or rescuing victims of the slave trade. Money is needed to accomplish all of it. The Kings & Wealth conferences require funding. Thankfully, God has given me the ability to self-fund the conferences, at least for these early years.

Kings honor God by funneling wealth into the kingdom. Kings are called to be kingdom funders. In Acts 16, Lydia, a wealthy merchant of expensive purple dye used in royal clothing, was able to house Paul and the other missionaries. When Paul stayed with her, she and her household were baptized (Acts 16:15). She became the first European convert. In the Old Testament, there was never any question that kings like David, Solomon, and Hezekiah were to use their wealth to build or restore the temple. Kings today honor God when they do the same. Kings themselves must therefore get to the place of overflow and abundant provision. It becomes exceedingly easy to fund and accomplish any mission when kings live from the place of provision.

Recently I came across two kings who struck a chord deep within me. They have these common denominators: wealth and influence reaching beyond borders and generations, and a clear sense of serving God's purpose with their wealth and influence.

The first is an icon of our time, Kanye West, billionaire rapper, record producer, and fashion designer with tie-ups with major sporting corporations. Unless you have been living under a rock these past twenty years, everyone has pretty much heard of Ye and the controversies he has been embroiled in, not unusual for a public figure of his stature. He publicly proclaimed himself to be a born-again believer of Christ in recent years. This was reported in an online article:

> **"I'm definitely born again," West said. "When you're not in service to God, you can end up being in service to everything else."[3]**

This profound statement was made by a person who knows his existential purpose intimately, i.e., to serve God. And the fact is he is not just any person. His 2019 video "Follow God," featuring him and his dad, has 47 million views and almost a million likes.[4] His lyrics referencing his dad and what it means for him to be Christlike move millions in a direction towards God. My seventeen-year-old son has never been a big fan of Christian hits. Admittedly, his lack of interest is due to hearing it ad nauseam at home since I play worship music compulsively. But Kanye West doing Christian rap has intrigued and attracted him to no end. I am thankful for God's choice of a wealthy and influential king who can touch the hearts of Gen Z.

The second king is a pioneer and business titan I learned about through a personal acquaintance of mine. Thomas Maclellan, a successful banker in the 1800s, penned a covenant with God in these words on June 7, 1857:

> I renounce all former lords that have had dominion over me and consecrate all that I am and all that I have, the faculties of my mind, the members of my body, my worldly possessions, my time, and my influence over others, all to be used entirely for Thy glory and resolutely employed in obedience to Thy commands as long as Thou continuest me in life.[5]

Thirty-five years later, Thomas Maclellan moved to Chattanooga, Tennessee, and invested in an insurance startup called Providence Insurance Company that served blue-collar workers like coal miners. In 1910, the company went public.[6] Provident went on to become a multi-billion-dollar insurance group in the last century before it merged with another multi-billion dollar insurance group in 2000.[7]

Midway through the twentieth century, however, when they were nowhere near the mammoth corporation they became by 2000, they started a foundation with the family's name, the Maclellan Foundation. After their first meeting the foundation gave away $700 to local causes, including the Public School Bible Committee. Four generations later, the foundation's giving and grant making had snowballed into $600 million in total giving, equating to $925 million in present value.[8] I recently had the opportunity to speak with Daryl Heald, who married a Maclellan descendant and has been closely involved with the family foundation's work these past decades, in particular the generosity movement. I was profoundly impacted by Daryl's numerous weighty nuggets in our conversation, but this was by far my favorite: "Use worldly wealth to lay up treasures in heaven. Be smart and shrewd about it."

My point is this: What if we also are intentional and purposeful in building wealth? What heights can we reach? How many generations beyond ours can we touch? What if we no longer accumulate to titillate but accumulate to replicate?

The purpose and vision of my family embarking on real estate investing were revealed to me more than ten years ago. The first sparks came through an old series of sermons by my apostle and spiritual dad, Ryan LeStrange. In fact, I found his 2013 resource, including handwritten notes to ministry partners, where he wrote, "Provision is assigned to vision!"[9] What a powerful revelation!

The purpose of our family's real estate endeavors was always threefold:

1. Build wealth, enjoy financial freedom, and leave an inheritance and legacy for our descendants.

2. Take territory literally through the acquisition of real estate and thereby manifest God's kingdom in the natural. Recently, the Holy Spirit brought me back to an all-too-familiar passage and made me read it literally and through the lens of real estate. Suddenly, a once-tired passage turned combustible and was infinite with possibilities, such as my venturing across the Atlantic to buy properties in Texas! Let's see if you would view this passage differently:

Enlarge the place of your tent, and let them stretch out the curtains of your dwellings; do not spare; lengthen your cords, and strengthen your stakes, for you shall expand to the right and to the left, and your descendants will inherit the nations, and make the desolate cities inhabited.

—ISAIAH 54:2–3

3. Take God's mandate of restoration spelled out in Isaiah 58:12 literally and live it out in the natural.

Those from among you shall build the old waste places; you shall raise up the foundations of many generations;

> **and you shall be called the Repairer of the Breach, the Restorer of Streets to Dwell In.**
>
> —Isaiah 58:12

These passages empowered me to start a real estate business remodeling small, distressed apartments in Frankfurt with the vision to bring transformation to properties. My apartments were not only remodeled with excellence but with buckets of blood, sweat, and tears. I was able to unleash my creativity, keen eye for detail and aesthetics, and most importantly, my sense of sourcing properties that can be transformed into enviable profit. German buyers loved my turnkey properties. We sold our first flip to a single mom who fell in love with my apartment when she laid eyes on it. She was so thankful that we sold our property to her, albeit at above market pricing.

We also built a portfolio of rental properties over the years. My smallest rental property came through a Holy Spirit intervention in 2012. A close friend who was a working single mom got thrown by her landlord along with her daughter due to rents rising dramatically in our city then. They were sleeping on her ex's couch for months. I wanted to help, but I knew it was too much of an ask from my late husband. Apart from relating to him what happened to my friend, I kept to myself my desire to buy an apartment to house her and her daughter and still collect reliable rent that would be paid for her by the city. My husband and I were having a conversation about buying real estate over Christmas 2012. Out of the blue, he blurted out, "Let's buy a small apartment for your friend, and we can have a reliable source of rental income from the city council." We went on to acquire a tiny two-bedroom that not only yielded steady cash flow but has almost doubled in value since. The latest renters are finally fitting the profile that I have always desired: a young evangelist-pastor couple starting out in the city, who were so grateful to get the lease and who on their own accord decided to pay a whole year's rent upfront. Time and again

God used our real estate to be a blessing to others even though we didn't plan it as such.

Deuteronomy 8:18 reveals His purpose of giving us the ability to attain wealth—to establish His covenant. In fact, He commands that we should always remember that. I believe it is precisely because God wants to establish His covenant that His purposes and mine are intimately intertwined. I am an investor empowered by God, representing His kingdom, and having resources flowing through my hands to fund God's missions, be it missions in far flung corners of the world, feeding the poor, housing pastors, creating beautiful homes that transform communities, or investing in tech startups that will change people's lives for the better. All these accomplishments reveal His glory and establish His covenant on earth as I continually point to Him in all that I do.

Know your God-given purpose and assignment. Wealth can become a weapon of influence and an agent of change for the good. Jesus said in Matthew 6:24, "You cannot serve God and mammon." Otherwise, as Kanye West said in the interview, "When you're not in service to God, you can end up being in service to everything else."[10]

CHAPTER 10

Work Your Hands to Create Wealth

God has given you the power to get wealth. He will bless the work of your hands. So put your hands to work and get it!

Before we embark on the topic of wealth creation, we need to tackle a few common misconceptions that have been planted by false teaching and have infected believers everywhere. We need to remove the mental hurdles to making money in the first place. Here are some familiar instances.

Money Is the Root of all Evil

Money is often wrongly quoted as the root of all evil. The verse in question says:

> For the *love* of money is a root of all kinds of evil, for which
> some have strayed from the faith in their greediness, and

> pierced themselves through with many sorrows. But you,
> O man of God, flee these things.
>
> —1 Timothy 6:10–11, emphasis added

It is the *love* of money that leads to compromise, sin consequences, and sorrows. It is falling in love with money, having an insatiable appetite for money itself, that will destroy us. Money is defined by *Encyclopedia Britannica* as "a commodity accepted by general consent as a medium of economic exchange…in which prices and values are expressed.…It is the principal measure of wealth."[1] In other words, money is simply an economic tool, a work tool for us to achieve our objectives. It is the emotion and value that we attach to money that will get us in trouble. If we grasp the concept that money is a tool that can serve our purposes, specifically kingdom purposes, we will master money. We will have the ability to harness money to work for us. Conversely, if we fail to master money, money will master us. Didn't Jesus lay it out plainly in Matthew 6:24?

> No one can serve two masters; for either he will hate the one and love the other, or else he will be loyal to the one and despise the other. You cannot serve God and mammon.

In that same chapter He went on to say that we are not to worry about what we eat or drink and so forth. That, I believe, is His way of saying don't overvalue such things until you lose sight of what is truly important: things of God, your relationship to Him, and His kingdom. This in turn clarifies His statements in verses 32 and 33 of the same chapter immensely:

> For your heavenly Father knows that you need all these things. But seek first the kingdom of God and His righteousness, and all these things shall be added to you.
>
> —Matthew 6:32–33

How do we master money? I believe we must empower ourselves in the natural with education and knowledge, be it learning a new trade, learning new skills to create new revenue, or learning how to invest. Specifically, when we invest, an inverse relationship is created between us and money; money starts working for us and not the other way around. We become the master of money.

God Doesn't Like Wealthy People, God Doesn't Want Us to Have Abundance, or Money is Dirty

People, believers or not, tend to have problems talking about money because in some odd, subliminal way, they believe that money is dirty or unholy. People of great wealth tend to be extremely discreet in talking about their own net worth or reluctant to share wealth-building secrets. Unfortunately, it doesn't help that they are being targeted in recent years due to the widening gap between the haves and have-nots.

Simultaneously, money and finances are topics that most pastors have neither the knowledge nor the courage to tackle from the pulpit and understandably avoid. However, out of necessity, they continue to raise funds from congregations without giving parishioners the tools to make money in the first place. This results in a self-perpetuating cycle of believers feeling guilty making money and giving money to churches out of guilt or manipulation. All this warped perception and understanding of wealth is not what God intended.

We already pointed out that God is the owner of all things and His covenant towards us is infinite. Therefore, it follows that the resources potentially available for us are infinite as well. Jesus Himself operated in exponential multiples, as demonstrated by His spectacular feeding miracles. How do you reconcile His nature and the scale of those miracles with the misconceptions that God doesn't like us to be wealthy or like wealthy people?

Those misconceptions are simply lies planted by the enemy in the minds of believers over centuries to keep them ignorant, fearful, and visionless.

Moreover, we were already introduced to Deuteronomy 8:18, which states categorically that it is God who gives us the power to get wealth. It is God Himself, not anyone else, not us, who gave us that power and ability.

First Timothy 6 provides an even more unambiguous explanation:

> **Command those who are rich in this present age not to be haughty, nor to trust in uncertain riches but in the living God, who gives us richly all things to enjoy. Let them do good, that they be rich in good works, ready to give, willing to share.**
>
> —1 TIMOTHY 6:17–18

Where does it say that we shouldn't be rich? In fact, it is saying the opposite—it is God who gives you not only the power to create wealth but also gives you richly all things to enjoy. When I first read that verse closely, I experienced instantaneous deliverance and freedom from guilt and condemnation attached to having wealth, simply on that scripture alone. God has given us the permission to enjoy all things, to have financial peace and freedom, and to get wealth. Of course, with wealth comes great responsibility to be rich in good works. But wouldn't you rather be called a philanthropist and not a pauper? I would!

There is a plethora of scriptures, from Jesus' words in John 10:10 to Paul in practically every chapter of the New Testament, that are on point. Zeroing in on just one, this is how Paul drove home his point in a letter to Corinthians:

And God is able to make all grace abound toward you, that you, always having all sufficiency in all things, may have an abundance for every good work.

—2 CORINTHIANS 9:8

The truth is God wants to bless you lavishly, on purpose, and *with* purpose. The word 'prosper' appears in as many as 95 passages in the Bible. Circling back, it was always His intent throughout time to prosper us and be lavish with us. He said it time and again through Moses in every single chapter of Deuteronomy. This still applies to believers today. Deuteronomy 28:12 then states:

The LORD will open to you His good treasure, the heavens, to give rain to your land in its season, and to bless all the work of your hand.

Coupling the above with Deuteronomy 8:18, if God has given me the power to get wealth and said He will bless the work of my hands, then I ought to work my hands hard. Since the day I got hold of these two promises, I haven't stopped running!

A key to creating provision, I believe, is to boldly follow your God-wired intuition and instincts. When nudged by the Holy Spirit, don't talk about it—jump all over it and execute!

Peter ran into Jesus at his workplace when he was fishing, and Jesus repeatedly used Peter's line of work to bring provision and profit. Jesus always knew where the provision was; He told Peter to cast the net on the side of the boat where the fish were teeming or which fish contained the coin to pay all of their taxes. But there were results because someone followed through, no matter how stupid he thought His directives were at the time!

It's the marriage of timing, opportunity, and courage to go after the odds! I believe God has deposited and wired in each of us instincts, intuition, and ability to *go get* that wealth that He has laid up for us individually. Jacob personified being opportunistic and was incredibly sharp at working his talents to multiply his uggo flocks that eventually prospered and outgrew Laban's. There have been countless times when I ignored the Holy Spirit's nudge and missed opportunities in the stock market. I can't even begin to recount how often I have second guessed, doubted my instincts, and suffered from analysis paralysis. However, the times that I have followed through, I have profited big time.

With the pandemic turning the world topsy-turvy and remote working now a secular trend—i.e., here to stay—many have forged new avenues of revenue. My apostle's digital business revenue through his online ministry exploded the past two years when people looked intensely to digital connections. I recall a sermon of his almost a decade ago about the river in the garden of Eden that became four riverheads, Pishon, Gihon, Hiddekel and the Euphrates (Gen. 2:10–14). My spiritual dad had a brilliant revelation that this was a picture of multiple streams, that is, multiple streams of income. That sparked an impetus within me to push my family into real estate, in retrospect a life-saving hedge to my late husband being the sole provider previously.

In today's gig economy, from everyone working a day job while working as a ride-share driver, it is commonplace to hustle different streams of income. It's a holy hustle to work hard and provide.

The pandemic-induced economy has also created new opportunities and businesses. E-commerce platforms for handcrafted supplies have boomed during the last two years with the lock downs, for instance, face masks with design. Another area of business that has boomed big time is the janitor's business. Who would have thought that cleaning and sanitizing would now be BIG business?

What about the impact of technology on the economy? You would think that automation and technology would be erasing jobs, but opportunities abound if you know where to look. One recent article in the *Wall Street Journal* detailed how the tech economy has created innumerable more jobs to be filled. Blue collar workers without college degrees are getting offers from tech companies to receive on-the-job training to transition to technology positions.[2] Miso Robotics, which I've invested in, is a case on point. Miso Robotics provides automation solutions and robots for the restaurant industry. It was commonly thought that robots would eradicate jobs for people, but the opposite is happening. Miso Robotics' robots take over extremely mundane and unpopular tasks, like frying, where there is a severe shortage of labor, while workers are being trained to man the automation and transitioning into tech workers. They also pointed out that there is going to be a 3.7 million labor shortfall in the future.[3]

Being in real estate also reminds me time and again how hot a commodity it is to be able to work with your hands, from carpentry to plumbing to roofing. The shortage of services is acute, pushing pricing to historical highs. Have you thought of going blue collar instead? If you have a passion for automobiles and can work with your hands, what's stopping you from starting an auto repair business that can make six figures eventually? How about rolling up your sleeves and helping people manage their properties and tenants? I will be the first to pay someone to administer my properties and keep my renters happy. What about getting that real estate license you always talked about? Realtors make the fastest, biggest bucks if you are willing to put in the hard work in the initial years. Are you prepared to pay the price? The payoff is immense in due time!

To authenticate God's promise that He has also given me power to get wealth, I started a side-hustle—trading. I taught myself how to trade, how to invest online by mom-multitasking—while doing chores in my kitchen and watching business news channels such as CNBC, which I kept running 24/7. I remember thinking to myself in 2016: I have a law degree, an entrepreneurial mindset, and good instincts for profit. If these guys can make so much money playing with numbers, I don't see why I can't do the same. I averaged 15 percent in after-tax profit in my first two years. In 2020, there was a massive market crash in March. I took huge losses but eventually clawed my way back to break even through aggressive trading. I ended 2020 by a return of 25 percent, with almost a half million dollars in after-tax profit. In 2021, my tech stocks took a huge hit, but I still managed to make over two hundred thousand in gross profit. With rising inflation and carnage in Ukraine, the markets have been tumultuous in 2022, and my tech stocks have been catastrophic thus far. However, the Lord revealed a strategy to pivot which I will elaborate shortly.

As I mentioned, diversifying, and creating multiple avenues of revenue is key, and the pandemic forced me to pivot and be open to entirely new business relationships that I would otherwise never have had but for the lockdown. People became very open to building connections online. I focused on relationship building with business partners I have never even met face to face but are several notches above my success level. I encountered uncommon favor with key finance and banking professionals. They extended investing opportunities to me that are typically reserved for select savvy millionaire clients. As a result, I could participate in bridge lending to film projects with A-list Hollywood names such as Robert De Niro and Shailene Woodley that were closed in three to four months and averaged 12–15 percent annualized return. What did Deuteronomy 28 say about us being lenders? Together with exclusive access to high-yield funds, I was able to create six figure *passive* (i.e., I don't have to lift a finger; money works for me) income for my family the last eighteen months. This avenue of revenue literally came out of nowhere; I was just being smart with people and monetizing relationship-building and network.

No one is more thankful than I am for heeding the Holy Spirit's agile leading to diversify and mitigate risks through new investing strategies. This is especially key when the stock markets are currently volatile and bearish. In mid-May 2022, I suddenly found myself in Dallas to inspect a property I succeeded in bringing under contract. While in the hotel room, I saw these words in my spirit: "SHIFT SEED from Wall Street to Dallas." I knew then it was a God confirmation to make such a bold move and buy a property priced at $1.625 million. On Monday, May 16, I moved quickly to liquidate over 80 percent of all my stock positions to raise cash to pay for the property while taking major losses. I was trembling in trepidation while doing so. Today at the time of writing, May 18, 2022, there was a crash in the stock market.[4] The Dow slid 1,100 points and had its worst day since 2020. I averted being caught in the crash because I followed the Spirit's leading and exited from the market on Monday. On the same day, I got a notificationr that a $200,000 construction bridge loan with $51,000 earnings will be returned to me in a few days. In addition to my amazement, another film-making studio bridge loan of $250,000 will be repaid with earnings around the same time. Three weeks later, I got an email that another fund where I had $500,000 invested, was closing and I was getting my money back pronto with earnings to boot. I certainly didn't see that one coming. In short, the million-dollar cash equity I invested in my Dallas property was returned to me within a month albeit from other unrelated sources. Sign that God was at work. Wait, there's more. My business affiliate whom I collaborate with in this private lending business, was not only facilitating behind the scenes the loan repayments but also was key in facilitating the closing of the fund. Believe it or not, my brilliant business affiliate has his base in Dallas. The Holy Spirit was right on target. His strategy for me to pivot to Dallas not only averted a financial disaster for me, but just as Jesus told Peter which side of the boat to cast the net or could call up the precise fish containing the coin, I was directed to my new sowing ground that is bursting forth with provision and harvest for shifting my seed.

Apropos the topic of working our hands, have we forgotten that Paul was a tent maker and dare I say a home builder? Yes, he was a home builder of his time, created income and fed himself, and did not rely solely on church giving. As I recall, he was adamant about his financial independence.

> For you yourselves know how you ought to follow us, for we were not disorderly among you; nor did we eat anyone's bread free of charge, but worked with labor and toil night and day, that we might not be a burden to any of you, not because we do not have authority, but to make ourselves an example of how you should follow us.

—2 Thessalonians 3:7–9

Even Jesus had a side gig—He was a carpenter remember? How amazing that He chose to work wood with His hands and not just wave a chair out of thin air since He could pull money out of a fish! Why? I believe He was modeling for us that there is great value in being adaptable, being agile, and having different skill sets because His promise is He gave us the power to *get* wealth. This meant that firstly, we would have to *go and get*, and He would bless all the work of our hands, but the hands must be working to start with!

All that said, I have one note of caution regarding multiple streams of income: don't start something new until you have already succeeded in one, or you will be bankrupt multiple ways instead of creating multiple streams. There is usually a rocky path to profitability that needs to be learned and conquered. There is a process to success. You can't fast track that process.

I will end with this:

> And you shall remember the Lord your God, for it is He who gives you power to get wealth that He may establish His covenant.

—Deuteronomy 8:18

CHAPTER 11

Steward Your Finances Faithfully and Shrewdly

How we steward this lifetime impacts our eternity.

Money has always been a touchy subject at the pulpit. But Jesus talked about money in eleven of His thirty-nine parables. Let's mine two familiar but key passages for fresh takeaways.

Matthew 25—Stewarding for Maximum Return

In Matthew 25, the master entrusted his goods to his servants to care for.

> To one he gave five talents, to another two, and to another one, to each according to his own ability.... Then he who had received the five talents went and traded with them, and made another five talents. And likewise he who had received two gained two more also. But he who

had received one went and dug in the ground, and hid his lord's money.

—MATTHEW 25:15–18

The parable of the talents in Matthew 25 is a glaring example of how we tend to skew what Jesus said. Jesus' use of the word *talents* was not referring to an ability or capability. He was talking literally about an enormous amount of money. Specifically, one talent was equivalent to six thousand denarii, which in turn was equivalent to sixteen years of wages back in Jesus' day. Alternatively, it would have been paid in seventy-five pounds of gold, which would be valued at $2.2 million at the time of writing. The servant given the least amount to manage was reprimanded by the master for doing nothing with it. In today's global economic climate of rapidly rising inflation, doing nothing with money is going to cost us dearly! I too would be livid if my financial advisor did nothing with the IRA fund I entrusted him with. I made the mistake of waiting far too long to put a pile of Euro cash to work. This year, 2022, the Euro depreciated 20% against the US dollar through the course of the year. Although I have made substantial investments in the US the past two years by utilizing my Euros, I was still too late in putting a cash pile of Euros to work, thereby losing 20% of their value simply due to inactivity or analysis paralysis, just like that last servant that failed to actively manage his one talent allocated to him by his master.

Fast forward to the end of the parable: Jesus branded the do-nothing servant "unprofitable" as well as "wicked and lazy" for falsely accusing his master as a coverup for not doing his job (vv. 26, 30). On the other hand, the other servants had "traded," which I understood as actively finding ways to increase value and managed to double the funds entrusted to them. They were rewarded with the lazy servant's share. This was Jesus' analysis:

For to everyone who has, more will be given, and he will have abundance; but from him who does not have, even what he has will be taken away. And cast the unprofitable servant into the outer darkness.

—MATTHEW 25:29

I recall thinking in my early Bible study days how harsh and unfair it was of the master to take from the one with least and give to another with more. I then realized I was viewing the passage with the handout mentality of scarcity. Instead, the one who brings results gets rewarded. He or she who brings home the bacon deserves to be rewarded because he or she earned it. This happens every day in the real world. We don't it question it at the workplace. Why do we then doubt Jesus' motives here?

Sadly, we see a socialist trend rising in our time, in which some are demanding a universal wage without having to work for it. Communism is being romanticized to younger generations even though history has proven its catastrophic failure time and again.

I believe Jesus' message in Matthew 25 is more literal than literary—we need to steward, or manage, our assets and possessions, including money, to bring about maximum return. This was already taught repeatedly in Proverbs, the following verse being highly representative:

Whoever gathers money little by little makes it grow.

—PROVERBS 13:11, NIV

Did you also notice that the successful servants delivered not only increase but a 100 percent return? These kinds of returns are outstanding outliers in the contemporary investing world, unless they are hedge fund managers, who are top-performing sharks in the industry. You probably know where I am heading with this. Doesn't Jesus sound like a shark too since He clearly favored those servants who doubled their funds?

On a more serious note, what do you think His expectations are of us then? What are we doing to create growth and increase of our money and material possessions? Will we manage to double what has been entrusted to us? Maybe not immediately but sometime in our lifetime?

As for me, I strategize 24/7 in my head how best to manage and optimize our family assets and to diversify investments to hunt for return, increase, and growth. It's like playing chess in my head all the time. The wheels in my head never stop turning. I pour immense time and energy into making connections in the investing world and scouring and vetting deals that I could back and seed for a tenfold return. They are like haystack needles. After all, Jesus Himself did promise hundredfold harvest for those who sow in good ground:

> **But these are the ones sown on good ground, those who hear the word, accept it, and bear fruit: some thirtyfold, some sixty, and some a hundred.**
>
> —Mark 4:20

We will examine closer in the next chapter how to get to that level of sowing, but for now, according to what Jesus has said, there seems to be no limit in the increase available for us.

Every investment decision is weighty, even scary at times, and requires a delicate balance of courage and careful consideration. Jesus did say in Luke 14:28 to "sit down and first count the cost" before contemplating building a tower. Throughout the process, I trust the Holy Spirit to order my steps and to open and shut doors as promised in Isaiah 22:22. Nevertheless, this decision making requires another key trait that is undervalued and has received a lot of bad press: being shrewd.

Luke 16—Stewarding Faithfully Yet Shrewdly

To make sound financial decisions, one must be shrewd—not

stingy, but shrewd. The word *shrewd* came from Jesus Himself! In Luke 16, Jesus related a parable of the servant who had been slacking off and knew he was going to be fired. So, he went ahead and collected some debts owed to his master by reducing the debts. In the process, he made friends out of the master's debtors, as they owed him one, proverbially speaking.

The master in the parable complimented his moves as smart, even though in some ways he could be seen as committing fraud by reducing the debts without the master's consent. The NLT version brings clarity to this passage:

> **The rich man had to admire the dishonest rascal for being so shrewd. And it is true that the children of this world are more shrewd in dealing with the world around them than are the children of the light. Here's the lesson: Use your worldly resources to benefit others and make friends. Then when your possessions are gone, they will welcome you to an eternal home. If you are faithful in little things, you will be faithful in large ones. But if you are dishonest in little things, you won't be honest with greater responsibilities. And if you are untrustworthy about worldly wealth, who will trust you with the true riches of heaven?**
>
> —LUKE 16:8–11, NLT

It's hard to understand at first glance, but Jesus was complimenting the servant's ability to capitalize on opportunities, and the servant did it in a way that benefited not only himself but others as well. In this case, the debtors benefited from his debt restructuring. Jesus pointed out that being smart with money is something that children of the light ought to learn. Why is being shrewd even necessary? Jesus said:

> Behold, I send you out as sheep in the midst of wolves.
> Therefore be wise as serpents and harmless as doves. But
> beware of men.

—MATTHEW 10:16–17

Jesus even said, in verse 12, if we can't even handle money or earthly treasures faithfully—that is, excellently—how can we be trusted with spiritual responsibilities that are of eternal value? Managing money well is a step to spiritual promotion. Who would have thought that Jesus said that? I didn't. What Jesus is saying contradicts what most in the church believe, including me, until I got hold of this truth myself. Jesus is requiring us to be shrewd—i.e., money smart, not just Bible smart—albeit with integrity, ethics, and honor.

> The one who faithfully manages the little he has been
> given will be promoted with greater responsibilities.

—LUKE 16:10, TPT

To conclude, I interpret Jesus' take on shrewdness to be having the ability to think critically and optimize a situation for one's benefit (for instance, always ask for a better price), as well as the benefit of others. It's called doing win-win deals. It's good business. As my friend Daryl Heald said, "Use worldly wealth to lay up treasures in heaven. Be smart and shrewd about it."

It also goes without saying that faithful stewardship extends to different crucial areas of our lives, not only finances. That's simply a foundational truth. This means we ought to steward our talents and abilities for kingdom purposes faithfully as well. One area close to my heart is faithful stewarding of time, which I touched on in chapter 3. It's an uphill challenge, but Ephesians 5:16 says we ought to redeem our time. When I look at my seventeen-year-old, I am choked with emotion wondering how a twenty-inch baby became six-foot-one and is moving to college on a different continent. We ought to do our best to make every day count. Our loved ones may not be around for as long as we want or hope. I know this firsthand with the unexpected passing of my husband. Only God knows how many mistakes I made in our time together. I can't undo the past mistakes, but to the best of my ability, I can make each day count.

When all is said and done, and you are standing before your Maker, He will want an account of how you managed the life He gave you. In that place where time no longer matters, the only thing that you would want to hear is this:

> **Well done good and faithful servant; you were faithful over a few things, I will make you ruler over many things. Enter into the joy of your lord.**
>
> —MATTHEW 25:21

You see, I believe our lifetimes are but a blip in the timeline of eternity. Not only that, but our lifetimes are also simply a gateway into God's eternity. *How we steward this lifetime impacts our eternity.* Our skills of stewarding money, assets, material possessions, all forms of earthly treasures, talents, time, people, connections, relationships, etc. are, however, developed and honed in this lifetime. In other words, we are in a pilot trial and are being prepped for commercial rollout—bigger and better things to rule over: the new Jerusalem, new cities. And who knows? Maybe even new planets in the universe! First Timothy 6:18–19 rounds this point up beautifully:

> **Let them…be rich in good works…storing up for themselves a good foundation for the time to come, that they may lay hold on eternal life.**

Practical Financial Tips for Life Application

This is essentially a book to transform and renew your mindset with words of life through biblical teaching backed up by powerful testimony. This is not a finance book. I would highly recommend Dave Ramsey as an authority on finance courses to get you into financial health. However, I am happy to share personal tips and insights that have been effective in our journey of wealth building.

Save! Practice delayed gratification.

Before we bought a house, we saved about 40 percent of the monthly household net income. By the time we owned a house, we had plenty of savings to gut and remodel our home extensively to create value without breaking the bank. We were ahead of schedule to pay down our house and built tremendous equity by the time I sold it.

We practiced fiscal discipline for years to achieve the dream of owning our home, which later mushroomed into a strong portfolio of real estate. Other families in our income category were buying yachts and planes or living the good life excessively, but we always kept our eye on the ball. We enjoyed luxury family vacations to create great memories for our children, but the expenditure was never overreaching. There was never a month that we had trouble paying bills. It was stunning for me to learn that as many as 60 percent of US consumers live from paycheck to paycheck.[1] Now with rapidly rising inflation and living costs, a paycheck-to-paycheck lifestyle is not going to cut it. Living below your potential is not God's plan for you. A financial overhaul is needed to get through the tough times!

In short, beef up your financial literacy. Live way below your means. Build a cash buffer. Create saving goals and keep track of spending by budgeting. Stave off purchases of nonessential items until they become truly essential. Limit the number of vacations in a year. Hopefully you have managed to save a bunch during the pandemic with restricted travel and not blown your savings on shopping online excessively! Hopefully, you saved like Joseph did for Egypt during the seven years of abundance as the lean years are around the corner.

Strive for unity in financial decisions.

Married couples, beware: a major key to tapping the wealth anointing is to achieve agreement in financial decisions. My late husband and I were both alphas, and it was a hard fight on many fronts, but in making investments and building a nest egg for our family, we could come to an agreement very easily. Over the years, we were stunned to see how God poured blessing after blessing on our joint financial decisions. The key is marital unity. God loves unity in marriages.

Pay down debt *except* in real estate acquisition.

We all know the weight of being heavily indebted. Student loans, credit card bills, car loans, mortgage payments—they all weigh on your peace of mind cumulatively. The average student loans in the US amount to almost $30,000 per person.[2] Debt is the number one reason why God's people are unable to prosper as God intended. They are held hostage by the enemy through lack and scarcity. Proverbs 22:7 says that "the borrower is servant to the lender." Romans 13:8 says, "Owe no one anything except to love one another." Finally, Deuteronomy 28:12 says, "You shall lend… but you shall not borrow."

My personal view on borrowing is this: I would prefer to pay upfront for things that are expendables—consumer goods that have no inherent or appreciation value. I would prefer not to borrow for my purchases. I simply don't buy if I can't afford it. As a single young person living in consumerist Hong Kong twenty-plus years ago, I lived the extravagant high life until I couldn't. I lost all my savings in the Asian financial crisis in 1998 when the stock market crashed. I became broke overnight and had to borrow from the bank to pay my taxes. Thank God for a high-paying attorney job to help pay my rent and start over! I didn't have a choice but to cut back drastically on my spending habits and transform my lifestyle. Those were hard lessons learned. Unlike me, you don't have to become broke overnight to learn good spending habits.

With the rise of financial apps on our phones, it is too easy to get credit lines to finance a lifestyle you cannot afford. The readily accessible buy-now-pay-later options when you make a purchase are enticing people into more and more debt. Every email and every ad is targeted at you due to automated, algorithmic tracking of every click and spend. Think before you click.

Credit card debt is very expensive and should always be the first to be paid down. The interest rates are already exorbitant at 16.4 percent,[3] but with rising borrowing costs, they will not stay at that level for long. Get rid of credit card debt *first*!

Only buy a car with monthly payments that are modest, and you can easily afford if you decide to finance it. We used to buy only secondhand cars with cash to get better bargains and not have another thing to pay for every month. I understand that this might not be a viable option for most but keep all purchases modest. Be mindful of car loans getting increasingly expensive. Don't splurge on luxury cars until you have succeeded.

The exception with our personal no-debt rule would be when it comes to buying properties. Although I agree that properties ought to be bought with financing, with the current rising interest rate environment, do proceed with caution. To assist, educate yourself on debt management. For example, follow the 28-percent rule, which is don't spend more than 28 percent of your gross monthly income on your mortgage payment.[4] Even that rule can be quickly eclipsed in current rising rate environments. A recent *Wall Street Journal* article states that "a median American household needed 34.2% of its gross income to cover mortgage payments on a median-priced home in January," up from 29 percent a year earlier.[5]

Fundamentally, I would recommend staying conservative on taking on debt so that debt doesn't master you. Having minimum debt in our family allowed us to sleep better at night. This has always been our strategy. Particularly, when it comes to your own residential home, keep debt levels low and light, and pay off the mortgage quick. This is because the residential property is not a revenue-generating asset. There are little to no tax benefits, such as deducting mortgage interest and property tax payments, etc. At this juncture, I would recommend you invest in financial education in your weaker areas to beef up your knowledge and your bank account.

Remember, steward finances shrewdly but faithfully, ethically, and always with integrity. How we steward this lifetime impacts our eternity.

CHAPTER 12

Sow with Strategy, Expect Return

You are not giving into a bottomless pit or a black hole, but sowing powerful seeds into infinite harvest and eternity

I have lost count of the number of fights my late husband and I had when it came to giving to the body of Christ during our seventeen years of marriage. I was sold into the strict doctrines of Malachi 3:8 against robbing God and therefore easily guilted into giving. God forbid, I steal a cent from an angry God and His wrath would rain down from heaven on our family and take everything we possess away in one fell swoop. Meanwhile, Mario was trying to be protective of what we had built out of the exact same fear. With his German upbringing and critical-thinking mindset, he questioned for years the manipulative methods many preachers use to raise funds on Christian TV or even in local churches. In hindsight, he was right on many counts about their flawed motives behind fundraising and poor stewardship of funds raised, but he was wrong when it came to his own personal motivation to withhold giving at all costs.

After a decade of wrestling, we found our middle and mutually agreed set of Biblical principles that worked for our family. These principles have yielded results and an amazing harvest over a decade through consistent application. They all can be grouped under the main theme of *sowing with strategy and expecting return*. There must be intentionality about giving; it must not be haphazard. The principles can be outlined as follows:

- Sow to honor, vision, and purpose.

- Sow in good soil, and expect seed multiplication.
- Sow seed with assignment, and expect fulfillment and return.
- Sow into the Abrahamic covenant.

The Elephant in the Room

Before I proceed to flesh out those principles, distilled and derived through years of struggle, I would like to address the elephant in the room—tithing. That was our number one area of dispute when it came to giving to the body of Christ. As a top performer and high earner who was extremely knowledgeable in the corporate world, my late husband was not about to release 10 percent of his annual salary to a local church. Looking back, he had very good reasons for his reluctance.

Firstly, he had witnessed horrific abuse by local clergy in the North German parish where he was born and raised. The pastor of the small local church not only fleeced the farming community parish by making outrageous demands on free goods and services using his position of influence but, finally and predictably, absconded with church funds. Understandably, that solidified distrust and even hatred within his family of the church institution.

Secondly, 10 percent of his annual salary, gross or net, would have amounted to six figures on an annual basis, an astronomical amount by any stretch, and too much to ask of someone whose faith foundation was severely shaken and damaged by negative church experiences.

Finally, it would be an understatement to say that the money management skills of the local clergy were severely inadequate. His lack of confidence was not unjustifiable, considering the pastor of the local church we were at for eleven years refused to have anything to do with church finances, saying that it would somehow distract him from his pastoral duties or worse, taint him. This is tantamount to the CEO of a corporation saying he has no clue of the numbers in his business and yet demand shareholder confidence in leadership. To make matters worse, we sat through an entire church membership meeting only to confirm our worst fears: there was excess and waste in fund utilization on multiple fronts. At around the same time, a scandal broke out in Singapore about how the leadership of a mega church, including the senior pastor, was charged with misuse and misappropriation of church funds to the tune of 50 million Singapore dollars.[1] All of this had impacted our thought process on giving.

And so we decided in unison not to give 10 percent of our household income, and not to give only to our local church but to spread giving over different ministries in the kingdom. However, to be clear, our annual giving for several years averaged out to be as much as the annual household income of a German family, which is approximately $50,000 a year. In fact, we maxed out the 20 percent limit that can be deducted as expenses for charitable donations under German tax laws. Our German accountant was so alarmed, he remarked we were "giving too much," to which my husband replied, "None of your business!"

Before I share our thought process on this highly combustible issue, please note my disclaimer at this juncture—I am merely sharing my personal insights on what worked for us. You must do what you think is right. We gave on the basis on our beliefs and what was right for our family.

Let me share our line of thought beginning with why God wants us to give in the first place. I firmly believe the following takes place when we give:

It frees us of mammon bondage.

Jesus said unequivocally in Matthew 6:24 that you cannot serve God and mammon. The fundamental question is, do we place our trust in Him or in earthly riches? That was the issue that Jesus was trying to confront the rich young ruler with, when He asked him in Matthew 19:21 to sell what he had, give to the poor to have treasure in heaven, and follow Him. Jesus knew that young man had placed his salvation in his riches and not in Jesus. This was confirmed through Jesus' challenge to him. It wasn't about his wealth; it was about his *trust*.

In order to not be slaves to mammon, we need to constantly ask ourselves, do we trust Him or earthly riches? What do we fear losing more? How do we prove that our trust is in Him? We give generously as led, and yet we have the freedom to withhold *without* fear of reprisal by God. God doesn't need our giving; we do.

The rest of our wealth and material possessions is sanctified and blessed when we give a portion thereof in generosity.

In one of his letters, the apostle Paul wrote:

And since Abraham and the other patriarchs were holy, their descendants will also be holy—just as the entire batch of dough is holy because the portion given as an offering is holy. For if the roots of the tree are holy, the branches will be, too.

—ROMANS 11:16, NLT

To that end, isn't it a given to want all your wealth and material possessions to be blessed and sanctified by the Lord? Isn't it then a no brainer to give a portion so that the rest is sanctified?

Fundamentally we agree on giving, and we wanted to give, just *not* tithe strictly according to Old Testament law. Touting Malachi 3 that we are robbing God and punitive consequences will follow is so wrong on so many levels. It's Old Testament. We are under the new covenant. Therefore, the New Testament should govern our giving and not the old. Our family finally found peace and agreement in 2 Corinthians 9:6–7:

> **But this I say: He who sows sparingly will also reap sparingly, and he who sows bountifully will also reap bountifully. So let each one give as he purposes in his heart, not grudgingly or of necessity; for God loves a cheerful giver.**
>
> —2 CORINTHIANS 9:6-7

That settled the issue for us! We decided to go with the standard of the *cheerful giver*, to give joyfully. Until the present, even with my husband no longer present, I am firmly convicted that 2 Corinthians 9 governs the new standard for giving under our new covenant relationship with Christ—that of a *cheerful giver*!

It is wrong to pressure, guilt, and manipulate people into giving by any stretch. It makes people vulnerable to abuse when there is no room to challenge demands on giving. As good stewards, we ought to discern when demands on giving are manipulative and controlling. Or have we no need for discernment when it comes to church giving? Is there a blind spot when it comes to giving that I am unaware of? I must have missed that memo!

The more relevant question is, are we giving out of fear or faith? Are we operating in legalism or agreement with God's Word? We ought to be cheerful givers as we purpose in our hearts—nothing more, nothing less. It's as simple as that. Before my family came to agree on tithing, we were either giving too little out of fear or too much out of fear of displeasing God. Either way it was motivated by fear and not faith. Once we agreed and were in unity, we saw God's blessing on each decision. It was never about the amount; it was about our personal motivations on giving. That's why Jesus praised the poor widow's offering of two mites, or small copper coins.

In addition, another powerful principle kicks in when we choose to go against our fleshly instinct to guard ourselves financially. Man's base instinct to be safe and have financial security is threatened when money is given or taken away. But this is precisely what is required of us in order that mammon has no hold of us. The result of us acting counterintuitively is nothing short of being miraculous. The Passion Translation of 2 Corinthians 9:6–8 states it lucidly and joyfully to the point of being infectious:

> A stingy sower will reap a meager harvest, but the one who sows from a generous spirit will reap an abundant harvest. Let giving flow from your heart, not from a sense of religious duty. Let it spring freely from the joy of giving—all because God loves hilarious generosity! Yes, God is more than ready to overwhelm you with every form of grace, so that you will have more than enough of everything—every moment and in every way. He will make you overflow with abundance in every good thing you do.

In our family, as we continued to give generously, cheerfully, and joyfully without major dissension or dispute, we kept on prospering in all our financial decisions.

Moving on, we realized more and more that giving was not just giving into a bottomless pit or a black hole, but it was to be viewed as sowing—sowing powerful seeds into the ground of the spiritual realm.

Sow to Honor, Vision, and Purpose

As I mentioned earlier, for years I was guilted into giving. However, God never intended giving to be an act of guilt but an act of honor to Him and His kingdom.

Proverbs 3:9–10 (NLT) states:

> **Honor the LORD with your wealth and with the best part of everything you produce. Then He will fill your barns with grain, and your vats will overflow with good wine.**

The objective is to *honor* the Lord with our best, not to focus on the latter part of the verse: that He wants to fill your barns with grain.

We are to honor God with our wealth and with the best part of everything that we can offer Him. The focus is *not* the quantity but the quality of our offering. That was precisely Cain's problem.

My most precious commodity is not money but time and effort. Doing Kings & Wealth conferences and ministering to kings is my best offering to the kingdom, my definition of firstfruits. It costs me immensely timewise, emotionally, mentally, intellectually, and finally, financially to communicate the message God has given me to call out and raise kings from the body of Christ. It would have been infinitely easier to throw money at other ministries doing kingdom work that is somewhat aligned. But the message of kings is what God has given me, Wai-yee Schmidt, to steward. Should I delegate my calling because it's inconvenient? I, for one, will steward to the best of my ability, albeit imperfectly, what I have been given. I know I am honoring God with my heartfelt endeavors, blood, sweat, and tears, and I will not circumvent all of it by simply throwing money at causes.

What's your best gift that you can honor Him with?

Secondly, seed sowing is critical in honoring the ministries that you have sat under. There is a core group of ministries that I have sat under for a long time, as their teachings have been instrumental in my growth. I have supported and honored these ministers through consistent seed sowing over a twelve-year period.

My main source of spiritual covering is being under the spiritual authority of my apostle and spiritual dad, Ryan LeStrange. I have sowed financially into him and his ministry activities for more than ten years. I have not only benefitted from his powerful teachings and revelations on the apostolic and prophetic and heaven's economy, but I also have received unquantifiable yet tangible blessings of being under his spiritual covering. I have no doubt that we have also flourished financially as a family because of this precious covenant relationship.

I also sow regularly into other powerful ministries to honor them and their respective teachings that have impacted and shaped me profoundly in countless ways. To name a few great men and women of God that I love sowing into, they include David Herzog, Sid Roth, Andrew Wommack, Lance Wallnau, and Joyce Meyer.

As we sow, we not only honor these great men and women of God, but we are sowing into their respective powerful assignments, visions, and purposes, as well as their harvests. It's not unlike buying shares in the company whose products you consume and therefore believe in, for instance, Apple.

Have you honored the ministers who have invested and poured into your growth? As you step up in faith to sow and bless them, you will partake in their unique assignment and harvest.

Sowing in Good Soil, and Expect Seed Multiplication

Mark 4:1–20 contains one of the most illuminating teachings on sowing, as it portrays clearly the laws set in place when God created the universe, the laws of seedtime and harvest. It's life changing when we begin to understand and apply these principles. Andrew Wommack's teaching on Mark 4 is one of the best I have heard, and I would recommend getting his materials for a deep dive in this area. Meanwhile, I'll share with you my simplistic take here.

To summarize, seeds that fell by the wayside were devoured by the birds. Seeds that fell on stony ground had no root and withered away. Seed that fell among thorns ended up being choked. All three instances were similarly unfruitful. For me, this chapter applies not only to the sending of the Word of God as gospel seeds falling on unfruitful ground, but it is also applicable to financial seeds.

As mentioned, I gave out of blind faith and guilt for many years, causing immense friction in my marriage. One instance that continues to sear my memory is when I decided to leave the American church we were with for eleven years and move to a local German church. As a parting gift, I wanted to bless the pastor and his family with €3,000 regardless of some theological differences between us. When I discussed this at that time with my husband, he immediately retorted that we would be sowing in bad soil since we were leaving the church, it was beyond clear that we weren't getting fed there, their views on money and wealth were not aligned with ours, yada, yada, yada, the list goes on.

Firstly, I was stunned by the revelation my husband had. It was spot on. Secondly, I decided to proceed, as the Lord showed me that we need to distinguish between giving and sowing. This was a case of giving not sowing—an act of compassion to bless others in need without any expectation of return. I went ahead and gave the money to the pastor. Half an hour later, his wife came running after me on the church premises and said the gift was a timely answer to their prayers. They were bound for a mission trip and had no provision for it whatsoever.

Through this incident, I took away two lessons: always check the quality of soil, and differentiate sowing with giving on compassionate grounds.

Circling back to Mark 4, Jesus said:

> **But other seed fell on good ground and yielded a crop that sprang up, increased and produced: some thirtyfold, some sixty and some a hundredfold.**
>
> —Mark 4:8

> **But these are the ones sown on good ground, those who hear the word, accept it, and bear fruit: some thirtyfold, some sixty, and some a hundred.**
>
> —Mark 4:20

I can't speak to the mathematical definition of a hundredfold, but one thing I know is it is an exponential multiple that Jesus was referring to. The point is that when seeds are sown in good ground, we can expect the seeds to multiply to as much as a hundredfold!

I arrived in this country with a $50,000 check, what was my lifetime savings twenty-two years ago, after grinding it out for seven years as a young law associate in Hong Kong. This sounds hard, but numbers don't lie. Twenty years later, I have seen a minimum of 20,000 percent return of that seed. Full disclosure—at that time and for a long time, I never saw it as a seed sown in good soil. But it was. Once the laws God set in place have been triggered, the forward motion can't be stopped. This is part of God's covenant with creation:

> **While the earth remains, seedtime and harvest, cold and heat, winter and summer, and day and night shall not cease.**
>
> —Genesis 8:22

Combined with Isaiah 55:10 (a frequently overlooked verse compared to Isaiah 55:11), we see it has always been God's full intention to give seed to the sower and multiply the seed:

> **For as the rain comes down, and the snow from heaven, and do not return there, but water the earth, and make it bring forth and bud, that it may give seed to the sower and bread to the eater, so shall My word be that goes forth from My mouth; it shall not return to Me void, but it shall accomplish what I please, and it shall prosper in the thing for which I sent it.**
>
> —Isaiah 55:10–11

Once a seed is sown in good soil, it will bring forth and bud. It will prosper in the thing for which it was sent, just like God's infallible Word, which He watches over to perform. A seed is like God's Word, and God's Word is like a seed; both will accomplish God's will. What a powerful metaphor by the prophet Isaiah! If you recall, I was directed to *shift* seed in a big way to Dallas. I can't wait to experience the exponential multiple He has in store for me there.

Finally, circling back to 2 Corinthians 9:10, all doubt should be removed when it comes to God's intention to multiply a seed when we sow it in good ground. Again, I prefer the TPT version that is not only lucid but positively infectious:

> **This generous God who supplies abundant seed for the farmer, which becomes bread for our meals, is even more extravagant toward you. First he supplies every need, plus more. Then he multiplies the seed as you sow it, so that the harvest of your generosity will grow.**

To recap, you are sowing, not just giving. Your seed will by virtue of God's laws and intent be multiplied as you sow. Furthermore, His laws of seedtime and harvest are as sure as the seasons and His sent Word.

This brings us to a critical inflection point—God's laws of seed-time and harvest and seed sowing have long been revealed and manifested in the natural, secular world of investing. That is why I invest. I want those same spiritual laws to kick in with my investments in the natural. Money invested in the secular realm is seed sown. Have you ever seen it from that perspective? Therefore, the secular venture capitalists often copy Biblical terminology, throwing terms like *seed funding* freely. In the investing context, if too much cash is left lying around uninvested, it is metaphorically referred to as dead money. Why? Wasn't it stated above in that passage that He multiplies the seed as you *sow* it? If you don't sow the seed, there is *no* seed to multiply and hence *no* harvest!

Venture capitalists and Wall Street fund managers seem to have understood and had success with Biblical principles of growth and multiplication without ever reading the Bible! Using Apple shares as a yardstick since it's a household name, did you know that if you invested $1,000 in Apple in 2011, the market value of your shares would have been worth almost $13,000 by August 2021?[2] That is more than an increase of more than ten times the original amount.

I am trying to play catch-up. As a matter of fact, and faith, I am expecting tenfold or twentyfold return from a few amazing tech companies where I have seeded investment capital, and it's not just talk. I am one of the top investors as well as a board advisor of Max Property Group, the owner of a European real estate crowdfunding platform called Max Crowdfund.[3] The platform has been growing phenomenally, and our aim is to get listed on the Amsterdam stock exchange in 2025. My six-figure seed investment in this group has already quadrupled in valuation within a year of being in the company. On a smaller scale, I have been blessed in the past with experiencing supernatural quick harvests, i.e., sowing and harvest reaping in accelerated time.

As mentioned, I have a core group of ministries I sow consistently and generously into that I deem not just good but fantastically fertile ground. I was traveling with David Herzog's Israel tour in 2018 when I sowed a four-figure seed on one of the days. A few hours later, back at the hotel, my stock portfolio popped in one holding, and I could take profit right away to cover my seed and more. On another occasion, in November 2020, I sowed a $10,000 seed into Sid Roth Ministries. The next day, one of my core stock holdings, Tesla, popped big time, and I could take profit right away—that seed had multiplied four times overnight. This happened several times the last few years.

To be clear, the quick harvests tend to relate to smaller amounts. The big money or harvests come through my real estate investments because of consistent seeding or investing over many years. Seedtime and harvest laws are laws God put in place that are inviolable, just like His Word.

Sow Seed with Assignment; Expect Fulfillment and Return

Giving your seed an assignment is one of the biggest lessons I have learned from Apostle Ryan. It's as easy to apply as it is effective. This is how I have taken this principle for myself and applied it. When you sow a seed, give the seed an assignment and declare a multiple-fold return to the level *your* faith will bring you—tenfold, sevenfold, thirtyfold, sixtyfold, hundredfold. For me, I like to start small, as you will see from my testimony below, and grow in my sowing as I grew in my faith.

Here are the instructions for sowing a seed with assignment:

- Be specific in framing the seed assignment.

- Place a demand on your seed and your covenant with God.

- Define your expected return or harvest.

- Be *bold*.

- Command the seed to fulfill the assignment in the name of Jesus.

- Exercise the authority you already have as a joint heir with Christ.

This is a fresh drop: Do you realize that the instructions detailed above are totally in line with Isaiah 55:11, which we analyzed previously? That is, a seed sent shall not return void, but shall accomplish and prosper in the thing it was sent for!

In December 2018, three weeks after my husband passed, I was supernaturally led by the Holy Spirit to buy an apartment, a luxury condo located in the heart of Frankfurt, prime real estate in our city. The decision was insane by any stretch and supernatural, but that is a story for another day. However, that December, a building fundraiser was started by the local church we were attending, Move Church. I purposed it in my heart to support the fundraiser and released a seed. I sowed a seed of €3,500 (about $4,000 at that time) and told the Lord *and* commanded the seed to *return* in the form of monthly rent in the amount of €3,500, without researching market rents at that time for that location.

To be candid, I was trembling with trepidation when I sowed that seed, as well as wrecked with grief and anxiety with the recent passing of the family's main provider. A few months later, I was right on the money when I signed the lease with a top bank executive paying me €3,500 a month for that apartment. In fact, I am paid all-in €4,100 monthly, and I am cash-flow positive on this property over $1,800 a month till this day. Since then, I have collected thirty-three months' worth of rental revenue, amounting to €135,000 before deducting mortgage payments and expenses. Pure profit amounts to approximately $60,000 for a $4,000 initial seed sown. The seed has multiplied over thirty times, brought in six-figure revenue to date, helped me pay my mortgage, and more.

It was a seed sown in good ground that fulfilled its assignment thirty times over and is still multiplying.

Another hot-off-the-press testimony -- on Pentecost week-end, few weeks ago before print, I sowed two seeds ($3000 and $12000) into Sid Roth's ministry organization with the respective assignments to call forth tenants for both my Austin and Dallas investment properties. Their prayer team said I will get my prayer answered in 21 days. In exactly 20 days thereafter, a tenant was confirmed for the Austin property for a monthly rental of $2900.

Sow Into the Abrahamic Covenant

Real estate has always evoked powerful emotions and instincts in me. I have always had a strong pull to real estate, even before I began in that industry as an investor. I have a keen sense of identifying properties well positioned to make money. I will pursue and nail those properties down. When I step into a space, I instinctively know how to add value to the property to prime it for high profitability. Window-dressing a property, like staging it, is something I can do in my sleep, and it's usually the icing on the cake after months of grueling remodeling that is as unglamorous as it is tedious. You can say that I am born with it, but I believe it's part of my new creation being, an anointing inherited through the Abrahamic covenant, which we are grafted into through our union with Christ.

If you recall, God said:

> I will make you a great nation; I will bless you and make your name great; and you shall be a blessing. I will bless those who bless you, and I will curse him who curses you; and in you all the families of the earth shall be blessed.

> —GENESIS 12:2–3

I will make you exceedingly fruitful.

—Genesis 17:6

Sowing into this covenant is literally idiot-proof guarantee to be positioned for an avalanche of blessings. What do I mean by that? You can never ever go wrong in focusing on blessing the Jewish people!

Notice that out of the core group of ministries that I regularly sow into, David Herzog, Sid Roth, and Lance Wallnau are all ministers with personal Jewish heritage. In fact, Sid Roth is what we call a Messianic believer, and his ministry focuses on reaching the Jews for Jesus first. Let's dig a little deeper here. Remember Jesus said He came for the Jews first in Matthews 15:24:

I was not sent except to the lost sheep of the house of Israel.

Paul subsequently provided the context excellently:

Did God's people stumble and fall beyond recovery? Of course not! They were disobedient, so God made salvation available to the Gentiles. But he wanted his own people to become jealous and claim it for themselves. Now if the Gentiles were enriched because the people of Israel turned down God's offer of salvation, think how much greater a blessing the world will share when they finally accept it.

Romans 11:11–12, NLT

The principle is simple. As they are God's chosen people, if they are blessed, everyone else is too; that is, the whole world is blessed as more and more Jews are reached and reconciled with their Messiah. This is the focus of ministers like Sid Roth, who teaches evangelizing the Jews first.[4] Essentially, there are extraordinary blessings laid up for those who evangelize the Jews. Another of my favorite ministries to sow into is an Israel-based and Israeli-led evangelistic organization called One for Israel.[5] They have been particularly successful within Israel in evangelizing the Israelis and Arabs using Hebrew and Arabic. I, too, have tried my hand personally to evangelize Jews in my city, to reconcile them with their Messiah Yeshua (Jesus in Hebrew). Invariably I tend to experience the quick harvest very often in connection with seeds sown into these ministries with a Jewish connection. Remember my latest testimonies on seeding in Sid Roth's organization?? Do you see the strategy behind this? When you sow into ministries reconciling Jews back to Jesus their Messiah, I believe the blessings that come forth are accelerated and multiplied.

In conjunction with blessing the Jews, another practice that has yielded immense fruitfulness is consistent seed sowing during specific timeframes, namely, during the Jewish feasts such as Passover, Rosh Hashanah, and Sukkot, the Feast of the Tabernacles, which is a particularly strategic time to sow since it relates to harvest. Some ministers call that aligning with God's calendar. Again, I believe the blessings that you can receive are accelerated and accentuated when you sow into these specific timeframes.

My personal path of blessing the Jews began very humbly years ago. After first learning about Genesis 12, I would push my stroller around the Jewish synagogues in my neighborhood when I took my toddler out for walks. Just like the Israelite nation taking the city of Jericho, I circled the synagogue repeatedly, prayed, and declared blessings over the Jewish people in my city. Subsequently, about twelve years ago, Christian TV network Daystar started broadcasting into Israel. I sowed a seed of $1,000 into it after pushing through—you guessed it—nuclear alert levels of tension with my late husband, who disdained certain personalities and manipulative fundraisers he saw on Christian TV. We came to a compromise when I explicitly agreed to only use my personal savings to sow the seed and not touch our joint savings. Right after, inexplicably Jewish connections and relationships suddenly appeared in our lives. Out of the blue my husband experienced tremendous favor with the most influential Jewish partners based out of the New York head office, who happen to be the kingmakers in their global firm. His career track became stellar, and he became the star of the European offices. Later, even he grudgingly acknowledged it was too much of a coincidence for all that to happen randomly and without godly intent.

In the years that followed, prime real estate was released from Jewish hands into ours. We bought our house from a Jewish Argentinean lady who went through a horde of aggressive, eager buyers only to reject every one of them but the Schmidts. Seven years later, the sale of my house broke records.

In 2016, we acquired a multifamily investment property that came through my investing and sowing into a seemingly insignificant friendship with a local Jewish baker, Tami. For years, I bought birthday cakes from this tiny bakery for my children's parties. Tami and I engaged in small talk but not more. One fateful day designed by God, I had the opportunity to talk to her an hour without a customer stepping into her usually busy store. Fully aware that she was from Israel, I shared the gospel with her openly. She was hooked and asked me to pray for God to forgive her. She was still five years away from officially acknowledging her Messiah, but on that fateful day, a multiyear friendship with my visiting her every other month and sharing Bible verses with her, specifically Messianic prophetic verses, had begun.

I then got acquainted with a realtor next to her shop. This realtor brought us a multifamily property owned by a very successful Jewish investor in the city. He initially declined our offer, as it was not the highest bid he could have received in our rising market. However, he was strangely persuaded by his business coach to take up our offer for a host of seemingly unrelated reasons that somehow made total sense to him, plus he couldn't help but take a liking to the Schmidts. Subsequently, I miraculously sold this property at the beginning of the pandemic at a price that made us more than half a million in profit after holding the property for only four years. In 2019 and 2020, as the world was plunged into economic crisis, I closed over $9 million in property sales alone.

By now you would have noted the other giant thread—real estate is a huge and natural part of Jewish heritage. As mentioned in chapter 1, Abraham was given the biggest land grant ever, i.e., Israel, which God gave him as an *everlasting possession*. In Psalm 37 alone, owning land is mentioned five times:

> **Those who wait on the LORD, they shall inherit the earth....The meek shall inherit the earth....Those blessed by Him shall inherit the earth....The righteous shall inherit the land....Wait on the LORD, and keep His way, and He shall exalt you to inherit the land.**

> —PSALM 37:9, 11, 22, 29, 34

Owning real estate is such a key aspect, it cannot be ignored! When we sow into the covenant, we will have the same harvests as Abraham did.

In the current environment, with rising interest rates, loans and mortgages have become much more expensive. However, my take is, with discernment, this could potentially be an opportunity to acquire properties as the inflationary environment means that the value of assets like real estate will rise along with inflation. If you don't aspire to own any property in your lifetime, you will miss out on capital and the price of assets appreciating over time. You will miss out on the opportunity to create wealth. In fact, it is not just an opportunity. It is your spiritual birthright. Don't miss out!

Another essential and overlooked component of the Abrahamic covenant is the finance anointing. The biggest banks in the world have Jewish names. In the Old Testament, God literally coached the Israelites how to conduct the lending business. They have a right to make money by charging interest on loans made to foreigners from as far back as thousands of years ago (Exod. 22:25). Today the biggest banks have Jewish names and founders. The head of the Rothschild clan, Mayer Amschel Rothschild, was born in a Jewish ghetto in Frankfurt in the 1700s.[6] The Rothschild family went on to develop the Rothschild banking business, which became an empire that stretched across the globe and across generations. Today, with an estimated secret wealth of $500 billion dollars and owning 1,800 properties spread across Europe plus significant stakes in major financial institutions (including the Bank of England), the Rothschild family is the richest family in the world.[7]

Friends, is it now apparent, the need to seed into the Abrahamic covenant, the anointing in real estate and finances? It is in the blood shed for us by Jesus. We are grafted into that anointing. And never forget to bless and sow into the Jewish people who are themselves His chosen and His beloved! For He will bless those who bless them.

Final Remarks

The war in Ukraine, rising global totalitarianism (not Russia ... think Canada's Trudeau freezing truckers' bank accounts over a peaceful protest in February this year!), the sharp rise in global inflation and borrowing interest rates, and disruptions in the workforce have made these years extremely tumultuous. There is talk everywhere of a global recession as economic growth slows due to central banks raising interest rates to dampen inflation. All of this is happening when many families are still trying to recover from two years of pandemic-lifestyle anomalies.

To me, war today is fought in the world of *finance* and *technology*. They are the battlegrounds. Financial weapons from crypto donations to economic sanctions to freezing of Russian bank accounts, etc. are weapons of war and are moving the needle. As of June 27, 2022, because of the economic sanctions, Russia is finally defaulting for the first time in 100 years on their sovereign debt. Is there any doubt that *wealth* is a *weapon of war* in our world today and we the Church need to have unlimited access to such weaponry and ammunition too??

There is no question that *kings* for Christ must arise and amass wealth. Kings must recover lost ground by taking back the leadership pinnacles of society so that God's dominion may be ushered in on earth. The ages darken as we speak. The ultimate war chest must be built in preparation for the end times that are shaping up before our very eyes.

We are standing at the precipice of an important era to witness a transfer in wealth and power. What is your role in all this?

Remember ... kings hold the keys. Kings must *arise*.

I'll see you at the next gathering of the kings.

Testimonies/Endorsements from 5 Alumni Kings

Annette Pacheco, a nurse from New Jersey, flew with bold faith to Frankfurt for the 2019 Kings & Wealth Conference. She caught hold of the Kings & Wealth teaching and ran with it. Not only was the king DNA in her awakened, but after she got back to New Jersey, doors opened supernaturally for her to start the process of opening an agency to provide health and social services. She has since been steadily building her business and now has a team of five employees. Her revenue has shot past $400,000 this year!

Minister Alan Marshall II of Alan Marshall Ministries wrote, "Wai-yee Schmidt carries an intense passion, dedication, and anointing to develop the body of Christ to function as kings in the kingdom of God. Her skills have led my family to pay off thousands in debt and form a business, and set the stage for me to become a lead consultant on a $64-million luxury apartment complex. More than ever ministers are stepping into the marketplace, where Schmidt's anointing is needed. She is not only a king but a prophet and a priest merging her talents, experience, and anointing while developing others along the way."

Apostle Chris White of Let Heaven Come Int'l Ministries in Belize wrote, "Before Kings & Wealth, there was a part of me that felt like answering the call to be a missionary and a minister was almost equivalent to taking a poverty vow. Wai-yee's revelatory teaching and mentorship destroyed that mindset and has awakened the King in me unlocking next Level, supernatural provision. Since then, God has unlocked previously untapped resources to invest in businesses that we are currently launching. We are starting a water filtration business that is being paid for an ex-weed farmer who gave his life to Jesus and handed his ill-gotten gains to us to finish building our filtration system. We are already getting customer inquiries from the government of a neighboring country to buy our water that could easily generate a few hundred dollars a day of revenue! The message of Kings & Wealth is equivalent to something from nothing or wealth creation at its finest."

After attending the Kings & Wealth 2020 Online Conference and getting hold of the Kings & Wealth message, Stéphanie of Montreal Canada, took personalized coaching lessons, allowing me, Wai-yee, to help her walk out her new identity and mindset of a king. All of 2021, I coached her in implementing some life-changing decisions. She not only became debt-free, but was able to sell her condo in Montreal at the right time and at market peak. Not only that, she was able to transfer her equity into a multi-family property to create rental income and enjoy capital appreciation. By the end of last year, she was so happy and exuberant about owning a revenue-creating real estate asset that she's now ready for more. Stéphanie is now building blocks of generational wealth for her family.

Shawn Stiteler, a successful roofing business owner in New Jersey wrote, "I was first introduced to Wai-yee Schmidt when I read an Elijah List article she wrote. For the first time I was finally reading something that put in words so well something that has been stirring in me for a few years now. Kings and Wealth! A message for men and woman of God who have been called into the market place and their role in God's eternal Kingdom. Shortly after reading this article, I saw an upcoming event she was hosting in Germany (half way around the world from me) and I knew I had to be there! This was a start of what has been a divine appointment. Wai-yee and her ministry Kings and Wealth is exactly what has been missing for KINGs to not only find their place and role in the Kingdom but to break out and thrive in their God-given assignment. If you feel called to business or called to help fund the Kingdom, then I can not encourage you enough to dive in and explore the hidden things that Wai-yee has uncovered in her journey with the Lord and lays out plain through the Kings and Wealth message!

About the Author

Wai-yee Schmidt is an attorney turned prolific global investor with a diversified multimillion portfolio of real estate, tech, and private equity investments, together with properties in US, Germany and Cayman Islands. As a major shareholder of EU property & fintech platform Maxcrowdfund.com, she is a member of their Board of Advisors. In addition, Wai-yee participates in exclusive private lending deals and wealth acceleration funds and connects high net worth individuals with wealth-building opportunities.

Wai-yee has been teaching God's Word the last 12 years with authenticity, passion, and powerful testimonies, focusing, the areas of kings' identity and wealth-building. Since 2018, she has founded and hosted Kings & Wealth conferences in Frankfurt, Belize and virtually, spearheading the Kings & Wealth message of mindset renewal, individual transformation, and church reformation.

Email the author: waiyeeschmidt@me.com

or stop by Facebook Page @Kings & Wealth, Instagram @kingsandwealthfounder and @kingsandwealth, YouTube channel Kings & Wealth or kingsontherise.com. The 2022 Kings & Wealth Conference video package is now available here:

kingsandwealth.com

URGENT PLEA!

Thank You For Reading My Book!
I really appreciate all of your feedback and
I love hearing what you have to say.

I need your input to make the next version of
this book and my future books better.

Please take two minutes now to leave a
helpful review on Amazon.com letting me
know what you thought of the book or go to
kingsontherise.com

Thanks so much!

Multiple blessings,
Wai-yee Schmidt

Notes

Introduction

Merriam-Webster, s.v. "groundswell," accessed October 21, 2020, https://www.merriam-webster.com/dictionary/groundswell.

[2] Wai-yee Schmidt, "The Transfer of Wealth, the Stock Market and the Clarion Call for the Body of Christ," Elijah List, January 17, 2018, https://www.elijahlist.com/mobile/display_word.html?ID=19527.

Chapter 1

[1] Bruce Wilson, "Lance Wallnau Explains the Seven Mountains Mandate," YouTube, July 16, 2009, https://www.youtube.com/watch?v=qQbGnJd9poc.

[2] Kayla Tausche, "White House Considering Tax Incentive for More Americans to Buy Stocks, Sources Say," CNBC, February 14, 2020, https://www.cnbc.com/2020/02/14/white-house-considering-tax-incentive-for-more-americans-to-buy-stocks.html.

[3] "Robinhood Raises $280 Million in Series F Funding Led by Sequoia," Robinhood, May 4, 2020, https://blog.robinhood.com/news/2020/5/4/robinhood-raises-280-million-in-series-f-funding-led-by-sequoia.

[4] Nicholas Abe, "Opinion: Robinhood Investors Are Beating the Stock Market—and Here's the Data That Proves It," MarketWatch, August 8, 2020, https://www.marketwatch.com/story/robinhood-investors-are-beating-the-stock-market-and-heres-the-data-that-proves-it-2020-08-06.

[5] Jonathan Garber, "Nasdaq Hits New Record, Briefly Crosses 10,000 for First Time," FOXBusiness, June 9, 2020, https://www.foxbusiness.com/markets/us-stocks-june-9-2020.

[6] "Homepage," Nasdaq, accessed December 9, 2020, https://www.nasdaq.com/.

[7] Schmidt, "The Transfer of Wealth, the Stock Market and the Clarion Call for the Body of Christ."

[8] Martha C. White, "Dow Closes Above 30,000 for First Time in History on Hopes of Economic Recovery Under Biden," NBC News, November 24, 2020, https://www.nbcnews.com/business/markets/dow-hits-30-000-start-transition-biden-prospect-yellen-treasury-n1247399.

Chapter 2

"Chinese Telecommunications Conglomerate Huawei and Subsidiaries Charged in Racketeering Conspiracy and Conspiracy to Steal Trade Secrets," US Department of Justice, February 13, 2020, https://www.justice.gov/opa/pr/chinese-telecommunications-conglomerate-huawei-and-subsidiaries-charged-racketeering.

[2] Blue Letter Bible, s.v. "*symphytos*," accessed October 23, 2020, https://www.blueletterbible.org/lang/lexicon/lexicon.cfm?Strongs=G4854&t=KJV.

[3] Blue Letter Bible, s.v. "*kabash*," accessed October 23, 2020, https://www.blueletterbible.org/lang/lexicon/lexicon.cfm?Strongs=H3533&t=KJV.

[4] Blue Letter Bible, s.v. "*radah*," accessed October 23, 2020, https://www.blueletterbible.org/lang/lexicon/lexicon.cfm?Strongs=H7287&t=KJV.

[5] Howard Gardner, *Frames of Mind: The Theory of Multiple Intelligences* (New York: Basic Books, 2011), xii, xiv, https://www.amazon.com/Frames-Mind-Theory-Multiple-Intelligences/dp/0465024335.

[6] *Where'd You Go, Bernadette*, directed by Richard Linklater (2019; Los Angeles: Annapurna Pictures, 2019).

[7] "WHO Coronavirus Disease (COVID-19) Dashboard," World Health Organization, updated October 27, 2020, https://covid19.who.int/.

[8] Stephanie Soucheray, "US Job Losses Due to COVID-19 Highest Since Great Depression," University of Minnesota Center for Infectious Disease Research and Policy, May 8, 2020, https://www.cidrap.umn.edu/news-perspective/2020/05/us-job-losses-due-covid-19-highest-great-depression.

Chapter 3

[1] Wai-yee Schmidt, "What God Wants to Do With These 3 Prophetic Types of Kings in This Hour," Charisma News, June 29, 2019, https://www.charismanews.com/opinion/76950-what-god-wants-to-do-with-these-3-prophetic-types-of-kings-in-this-hour.

[2] Elon Musk (@elonmusk), "I am an engineer," Twitter, July 8, 2018, 1:40 p.m., https://twitter.com/elonmusk/status/1016014090320338944.

[3] CNBC, "The Rise of Chick-fil-A," YouTube, August 29, 2019, https://www.youtube.com/watch?v=ZUdqlbQfWyg.

[4] CNBC, "The Rise of Chick-fil-A."

[5] John Eckhardt, *Deliverance and Spiritual Warfare Manual* (Lake Mary, FL: Charisma House, 2014), 144–155, 176–178, https://books.google.com/books?id=abDIAwAAQBAJ&vq.

[6] Julian E. Lange et al., "2018/2019 United States Report: Global Entrepreneurship Monitor," Babson, 2019, https://www.babson.edu/media/babson/assets/blank-center/GEM_USA_2018-2019.pdf?_ga=2.209966678.215739621.1604068909-254100770.1604068909.

[7] "Representation of Women and Minority Equity Partners Among Partners Little Changed in Recent Years," *NALP Bulletin*, April 2019, https://www.nalp.org/0419research.

Chapter 4

[1] Elon Musk, "Tesla stock price is too high imo," Twitter, May 1, 2020, 11:11 a.m., https://twitter.com/elonmusk/status/1256239815256797184?lang=en.

Chapter 5

[1] Evan Carmichael, "THIS is My BIGGEST SECRET to SUCCESS! | Warren Buffett | Top 10 Rules," YouTube, May 23, 2015, https://www.youtube.com/watch?v=iEgu6p_frmE.

[2] Katherine Rosman, "Bill Gates on Books and Blogging," *New York Times*, January 4, 2016, https://www.nytimes.com/2016/01/04/fashion/bill-gates-gates-notes-books.html.

3 Michael Simmons, "Why Constant Learners All Embrace the 5-Hour Rule," Michael Simmons LLC, accessed November 2, 2020, http://michaeldsimmons.com/why-constant-learners-all-embrace-the-5-hour-rule-mm09/.

4 Dan Moskowitz, "The 10 Richest People in the World," Investopedia, updated June 1, 2022, https://www.investopedia.com/articles/investing/012715/5-richest-people-world.asp.

5 Andrew Wommack, *Living in God's Best* (Tulsa, OK: Harrison House, 2017), chapter 8, https://www.google.com/books/edition/Living_in_God_s_Best/RPucDwAAQBAJ?hl=en&gbpv=0.

6 CNBC Television, "AMD CEO Lisa Su on second-quarter earnings and revised 2019 guidance," YouTube, July 31, 2019, https://www.youtube.com/watch?v=gf4g2PuRsOk.

7 Advanced Micro Devices, "Form 10-K," US Securities and Exchange Commission, February 4, 2020, https://www.sec.gov/ix?doc=/Archives/edgar/data/2488/000000248820000008/amdform10-kfy2019.htm.

8 "Advanced Micro Devices Inc.," *Wall Street Journal*, accessed June 7, 2022, https://www.wsj.com/market-data/quotes/AMD/historical-prices.

9 Jeffrey P. Bezos, "2017 Letter to Shareholders," Amazon, April 18, 2018, https://blog.aboutamazon.com/company-news/2017-letter-to-shareholders/.

Chapter 6

1 Blue Letter Bible, s.v. "*radah*."

2 "Apple Inc.," *Wall Street Journal*, accessed November 10, 2020, https://www.wsj.com/market-data/quotes/AAPL.

3 David Voreacos and Neil Weinberg, "Billionaire Robert Smith Admits Evading Taxes for Years," Bloomberg, updated October 16, 2020, https://www.bloomberg.com/news/articles/2020-10-15/billionaire-robert-smith-admits-he-cheated-on-taxes-for-15-years.

4 CNBC, "The Rise of Chick-fil-A."

Chapter 7

[1] First Chronicles 22:14 says "one hundred thousand talents of gold and one million talents of silver" were used. Using a sixty-six-pound talent, a gold price of $1,879.42 per ounce, and a silver price of $26.26 per ounce, the total is over $226 trillion.

[2] Neuralink, "Neuralink Progress Update, Summer 2020," YouTube, August 28, 2020, https://www.youtube.com/watch?v=DVvmgjBL74w&feature=youtu.be.

[3] Kelsey Piper, "The Case Against Colonizing Space to Save Humanity," Vox, October 22, 2018, https://www.vox.com/future-perfect/2018/10/22/17991736/jeff-bezos-elon-musk-colonizing-mars-moon-space-blue-origin-spacex.

[4] "The Bible App," YouVersion, accessed November 10, 2020, https://www.youversion.com/the-bible-app/.

[5] Lance Wallnau, "God Wants Nations," Lance Wallnau, November 1, 2015, https://lancewallnau.com/god-wants-nations/.

Chapter 8

[1] I recommend the *Moody Handbook of Theology* by Paul Enns as a resource about this.

[2] "The Richest People of All Time," Love Money, accessed April 21, 2022, https://www.lovemoney.com/gallerylist/51988/the-richest-people-of-all-time.

[3] "What Does It Mean That Jesus Had Nowhere to Lay His Head?," Got Questions, accessed April 21, 2022, https://www.gotquestions.org/nowhere-to-lay-His-head.html.

[4] Nathaniel Lee, "Warren Buffett Lives in a Modest House That's Worth .001% of His Total Wealth," Business Insider, updated November 10, 2020, https://www.businessinsider.com/warren-buffett-modest-home-bought-31500-looks-2017-6.

Chapter 9

[1] Investopedia Team, "Wealth," Investopedia, updated December 28,

2021, https://www.investopedia.com/terms/w/wealth.asp.

[2] Adam Hayes, "High-Net-Worth Individual (HNWI)," Investopedia, updated September 6, 2021, https://www.investopedia.com/terms/h/hnwi.asp.

[3] Molly Longman, "Kanye West Says Religion Saved Him From Alcohol," Refinery29, updated April 15, 2020, https://www.refinery29.com/en-us/2020/04/9693506/kanye-west-christian-religion-alcohol-addiction-gq.

[4] Kanye West, "Kanye West - Follow God," YouTube, November 8, 2019, https://www.youtube.com/watch?v=ivCY3Ec4iaU.

[5] Thomas Maclellan, "Our Covenant," Maclellan Foundation, June 7, 1857, https://maclellan.net/our-covenant.

[6] "Our History," Maclellan Foundation, accessed April 21, 2022, https://maclellan.net/our-history,

[7] Carol I. Keeley and Dave Mote, "UnumProvident Corporation," Encyclopedia.com, accessed April 21, 2022, https://www.encyclopedia.com/books/politics-and-business-magazines/unumprovident-corporation.

[8] "Our History," Maclellan Foundation.

[9] Ryan LeStrange, "Audio Collection with Handwritten Notes," 2013.

[10] Longman, "Kanye West Says Religion Saved Him From Alcohol."

Chapter 10

[1] Allan H. Meltzer, "Money," *Encyclopedia Britannica*, updated March 12, 2022, https://www.britannica.com/topic/money.

[2] Vanessa Fuhrmans and Kathryn Dill, "Blue-Collar Workers Make the Leap to Tech Jobs, No College Degree Necessary," *Wall Street Journal*, updated April 14, 2022, https://www.wsj.com/articles/tech-jobs-no-college-degree-necessary-11649371535.

[3] "Building the Kitchen of the Future," Miso Robotics, accessed April 22, 2022, https://waxinvest.com/projects/miso-robotics/.

[4] Orla McCaffrey and Caitlin Ostroff, "Dow Slides More Than 1,100 Points in Worst Day Since 2020," *Wall Street Journal*, updated May

18, 2022, https://www.wsj.com/articles/global-stocks-markets-dow-update-05-18-2022-11652859762?st=sk3cw43vqrogrz1&reflink=deskt opwebshare_permalink.

Chapter 11

Libby Cherry, "Why the Euro Has Tumbled to Parity Against the Dollar," Bloomberg, July 8, 2022, updated July 13, 2022, https://www.bloomberg.com/news/articles/2022-07-08/why-the-euro-has-tumbled-near-parity-to-the-us-dollar-quicktake

[1] Eric Rosenbaum, "As Inflation Bites and America's Mood Darkens, Higher-Income Consumers Are Cutting Back, Too," CNBC, updated April 9, 2022, https://www.cnbc.com/2022/04/08/as-inflation-bites-higher-income-consumers-are-cutting-back-too.html.
[2] Anna Helhoski and Ryan Lane, "Student Loan Debt Statistics: 2022," Nerdwallet, April 22, 2022, https://www.nerdwallet.com/article/loans/student-loans/student-loan-debt.
[3] Orla McCaffrey, Sam Goldfarb, and AnnaMaria Andriotis, "Interest-Rate Surge Ripples Through Economy, From Homes to Car Loans," Wall Street Journal, April 8, 2022, https://www.wsj.com/articles/interest-rate-surge-ripples-through-economy-from-homes-to-car-loans-11649426081.
[4] "What Percentage of Your Income Should Go Towards Your Mortgage," Chase, accessed April 22, 2022, https://www.chase.com/personal/mortgage/education/financing-a-home/what-percentage-income-towards-mortgage.
[5] McCaffrey, Goldfarb, and Andriotis, "Interest-Rate Surge Ripples Through Economy, From Homes to Car Loans."

Chapter 12

[1] "City Harvest Church Criminal Breach of Trust Case," Wikipedia, updated August 27, 2021, https://en.wikipedia.org/wiki/City_Harvest_Church_Criminal_Breach_of_Trust_Case.